THE
GREAT
CRASH
1929

Books by John Kenneth Galbraith

AMERICAN CAPITALISM: THE CONCEPT
OF COUNTERVAILING POWER

A THEORY OF PRICE CONTROL

THE AFFLUENT SOCIETY

THE SCOTCH

THE NEW INDUSTRIAL STATE

THE TRIUMPH

INDIAN PAINTING
(WITH MOHINDER SINGH RANDHAWA)

AMBASSADOR'S JOURNAL

ECONOMICS AND THE PUBLIC PURPOSE

MONEY: WHENCE IT CAME,
WHERE IT WENT

ANNALS OF AN ABIDING LIBERAL

A LIFE IN OUR TIMES

THE ANATOMY OF POWER

A VIEW FROM THE STANDS

ECONOMICS IN PERSPECTIVE:
A CRITICAL HISTORY

A TENURED PROFESSOR

THE CULTURE OF CONTENTMENT

A JOURNEY THROUGH ECONOMIC TIME:
A FIRSTHAND VIEW

THE GOOD SOCIETY:
THE HUMANE AGENDA

THE GREAT CRASH 1929

John Kenneth Galbraith

WITH A NEW INTRODUCTION
BY THE AUTHOR

A MARINER BOOK
HOUGHTON MIFFLIN COMPANY
Boston • New York

For information about permission to reproduce selections
from this book, write to Permissions, Houghton Mifflin Company,
215 Park Avenue South, New York, New York 10003.

Library of Congress Cataloging-in-Publication Data

Galbraith, John Kenneth.
The great crash, 1929 / John Kenneth Galbraith ;
with a new introduction by the author.
p. cm.
Includes index.
ISBN-13: 978-0-395-85999-5
ISBN-10: 0-395-85999-9
1. Depression—1929—United States.
2. Stock Market Crash, 1929. I. Title.
HB3717 1929.G32 1997   97-22051
338.5'4'097309043—dc21   CIP

Printed in the United States of America

QUF 19 18

Grateful acknowledgment is made to the publishers for
permission to quote from the following works: *Only Yesterday* by
Frederick Lewis Allen, published by Harper & Brothers, 1931.
Fluctuations in Income by Thomas Wilson, published by
the Pitman Publishing Corporation, 1948.

TO
CATHERINE ATWATER
GALBRAITH

Contents

The View from the Nineties

The Great Crash, 1929 was first published in 1955 and has been continuously in print ever since, a matter now of forty years and more. Authors (and publishers) being as they are, the tendency is to attribute this endurance to the excellence of the work. Evidently this book has some merit, but, for worse or perhaps better, there is another reason for its durability. Each time it has been about to pass from print and the bookstores, another speculative episode — another bubble or the ensuing misfortune — has stirred interest in the history of this, the great modern case of boom and collapse, which led on to an unforgiving depression.

One of the subsequent episodes occurred, in fact, as the book was coming from the printer. There was a small stock market boom in the spring of 1955; I was called to Washington to testify at a Senate hearing on the past experience. During my testimony that morning the stock market went suddenly south. I was blamed for the collapse, especially by those who were long in the market. A fair number of the latter wrote to threaten me with physical injury; a more devout citizenry told me they were praying for my ill health or early demise. A few days after my testimony I broke my leg while skiing in Vermont. The papers carried mention. Letters came in telling me of prayers that had been answered. I had at least done something for religion. In the mood of the times a senator from Indiana, Homer E. Capehart, said it was the work of a crypto-Communist.

That was only the beginning. The offshore-funds insanity of

the seventies, the big bust of 1987, less dramatic episodes or fears, all brought attention back to 1929 and kept the book in print. And so again now in 1997.

That we are having a major speculative splurge as this is written is obvious to anyone not captured by vacuous optimism. There is now far more money flowing into the stock markets than there is intelligence to guide it. There are many more mutual funds than there are financially acute, historically aware men and women to manage them. I am not given to prediction; one's foresight is forgotten, only one's errors are well remembered. But there is here a basic and recurrent process. It comes with rising prices, whether of stocks, real estate, works of art or anything else. This increase attracts attention and buyers, which produces the further effect of even higher prices. Expectations are thus justified by the very action that sends prices up. The process continues; optimism with its market effect is the order of the day. Prices go up even more. Then, for reasons that will endlessly be debated, comes the end. The descent is always more sudden than the increase; a balloon that has been punctured does not deflate in an orderly way.

To repeat, I make no prediction; I only observe that this phenomenon has manifested itself many times since 1637, when Dutch speculators saw tulip bulbs as their magic road to wealth, and 1720, when John Law brought presumptive wealth and then sudden poverty to Paris through the pursuit of gold, to this day undiscovered, in Louisiana. In these years also the great South Sea Bubble spread financial devastation in Britain.

Later there was more. In the United States in the nineteenth century there was a speculative splurge every twenty or thirty years. This was already a tradition, for the colonies, north and south, had experimented at no slight eventual cost with currency issues that had no visible backing. They did well until it was observed that there was nothing there. The Revolution was paid for with Continental notes, giving permanence to the phrase "not worth a Continental." In the years following the war of 1812–14, there was a major real estate boom; in the 1830s came wild speculation in canal and turnpike investment — internal improvements, they were termed. Along with this went issues of bank notes unbacked by anything of value and issued by anyone able to hire a building larger than that of the local blacksmith. This came powerfully to an end in 1837. In the 1850s came another boom and collapse, and in those years a New England bank, in a part of the country more cautious than most, closed down. It had $500,000 in notes outstanding and assets to cover them of $86.48.

After the Civil War came the railroad boom and a particularly painful collapse in 1873. Another boom came to an equally dramatic end in 1907, but the big New York banks were able, this time, to limit the damage. Earlier a considerable flow of British funds had fueled the American speculation, notably that just mentioned in railroads. There was also a renewed British involvement in South America, the South Sea Bubble now forgotten. The greatly distinguished Baring Brothers had to be rescued by the Bank of England from bankruptcy occasioned by its loans to Argentina. This is currently interesting, for in the 1990s Barings was caught up in the more or less incredible operations of one of its minor minions in Singapore. This time there was no rescue; Barings, for all public purposes, disappeared.

If we do now have a downturn — what is called a day of reckoning — some things can, indeed, be foreseen. By some estimates a quarter of all Americans, directly or indirectly, are in the stock market. Were there a bad slump, it would limit their expenditures, especially of durable goods, and put pressure on their very large credit card debt. The result would be a generally adverse effect on the economy. This would not be as painful as the aftereffects of 1929; then banks were fragile and without deposit insurance, farm markets were important and especially vulnerable, there was no cushioning effect from unemployment compensation, welfare payments and Social Security. All this is better now. But there could be a recession; that would be normal. There would also be, we may be certain, the traditional reassuring words from Washington. Always when markets are in trouble, the phrases are the same: "The economic situation is fundamentally sound" or simply "The fundamentals are good." All who hear these words should know that something is wrong.

Once more I do not predict and tell only what the past so vividly tells us. I offer a final word on this book. It was published in that spring of 1955 to an appreciative audience. There was a brief appearance on the best-seller lists; I looked with pleasure at the bookstore windows. On my frequent visits to New York, I was distressed, however, to see no sign of it in a small bookshop on the ramp leading down to the planes in the old La Guardia terminal. One night I stopped in to inspect the shelves. The lady in charge finally noticed me and asked what I sought. Somewhat embarrassed, I passed over the name of the author and said it was a work called *The Great Crash*. "Not a book you could sell in an airport," she responded firmly.

A Note on Sources

In recent times numerous authors and publishers have come to suppose that readers are offended by footnotes. I have no desire to offend or even in the slightest way to discourage any solvent customer, but I regard this supposition as silly. No literate person can possibly be disturbed by a little small type at the bottom of a page, and everyone, professional and lay reader alike, needs to know on occasion the credentials of a fact. Footnotes also provide an exceedingly good index of the care with which a subject has been researched.

However, there is also a line between adequacy and pedantry. In this book, where I have drawn on public documents, books, magazine articles, or special sources of any kind I have indicated the source. However, much of the story of 1929 is to be found in the general and financial press of the time. Systematic citation of these sources would involve endless references to the same papers. This I have not done. It means in general that if no source is given, the reader can assume it was in the *New York Times*, the *Wall Street Journal*, and the other papers of general circulation of the day.

THE
GREAT
CRASH
1929

———

CHAPTER I

"Vision and Boundless Hope and Optimism"

ON DECEMBER 4, 1928, President Coolidge sent his last message on the state of the Union to the reconvening Congress. Even the most melancholy congressman must have found reassurance in his words. "No Congress of the United States ever assembled, on surveying the state of the Union, has met with a more pleasing prospect than that which appears at the present time. In the domestic field there is tranquility and contentment . . . and the highest record of years of prosperity. In the foreign field there is peace, the goodwill which comes from mutual understanding . . ." He told the legislators that they and the country might "regard the present with satisfaction and anticipate the future with optimism." And breaking sharply with the most ancient of our political conventions, he omitted to attribute this well-being to the excellence of the administration which he headed. "The main source of these unexampled blessings lies in the integrity and character of the American people."

A whole generation of historians has assailed Coolidge for the superficial optimism which kept him from seeing that a great storm was brewing at home and also more distantly abroad. This is grossly unfair. It requires neither courage nor prescience to predict disaster. Courage is required of the man who, when things are good, says so. Historians rejoice in crucifying the false prophet of the millennium. They never dwell on the mistake of the man who wrongly predicted Armageddon.

There was much that was good about the world of which Coolidge spoke. True, as liberal misanthropes have insisted, the rich were getting richer much faster than the poor were getting less poor. The farmers were unhappy and had been ever since the depression of 1920–21 had cut farm prices sharply but left costs high. Black people in the South and white people in the southern Appalachians continued to dwell in hopeless poverty. Fine old-English houses with high gables, leaded glass, and well-simulated half-timbering were rising in the country club district, while farther in town one encountered the most noisome slums outside the Orient.

All this notwithstanding, the twenties in America were a very good time. Production and employment were high and rising. Wages were not going up much, but prices were stable. Although many people were still very poor, more people were comfortably well-off, well-to-do, or rich than ever before. Finally, American capitalism was undoubtedly in a lively phase. Between 1925 and 1929, the number of manufacturing establishments increased from 183,900 to 206,700; the value of their output rose from $60.8 billions to $68.0 billions.[1] The Federal Reserve index of industrial production which had averaged only 67 in 1921 (1923–25= 100) had risen to 110 by July 1928, and it reached 126 in June 1929.[2] In 1926, 4,301,000 automobiles were produced. Three years later, in 1929, production had increased by over a million to 5,358,000,[3] a figure which compares very decently with the 5,700,000 new car registrations of the opulent year of 1953. Business earnings were rising rapidly, and it was a good time to be in business. Indeed, even the most

[1] U.S. Department of Commerce, Bureau of the Census, *Statistical Abstract of the United States, 1944–45.*
[2] *Federal Reserve Bulletin,* December 1929.
[3] Thomas Wilson, *Fluctuations in Income and Employment,* 3rd ed. (New York: Pitman, 1948), p. 141.

jaundiced histories of the era concede, tacitly, that times were good, for they nearly all join in taxing Coolidge for his failure to see that they were too good to last.

This notion of an iron law of compensation — the notion that the ten good years of the twenties had to be paid for by the ten bad ones of the thirties — is one to which it will be worthwhile to return.

II

One thing in the twenties should have been visible even to Coolidge. It concerned the American people of whose character he had spoken so well. Along with the sterling qualities he praised, they were also displaying an inordinate desire to get rich quickly with a minimum of physical effort. The first striking manifestation of this personality trait was in Florida. There, in the mid-twenties, Miami, Miami Beach, Coral Gables, the East Coast as far north as Palm Beach, and the cities over on the Gulf had been struck by the great Florida real estate boom. The Florida boom contained all of the elements of the classic speculative bubble. There was the indispensable element of substance. Florida had a better winter climate than New York, Chicago, or Minneapolis. Higher incomes and better transportation were making it increasingly accessible to the frost-bound North. The time indeed was coming when the annual flight to the South would be as regular and impressive as the migrations of the Canada Goose.

On that indispensable element of fact men and women had proceeded to build a world of speculative make-believe. This is a world inhabited not by people who have to be persuaded to believe but by people who want an excuse to believe. In the case of Florida, they wanted to believe that the whole peninsula would soon be populated by the holiday-makers and the sun-worshippers of a new and remarkably indolent era. So great would be the crush that beaches, bogs, swamps, and common scrubland would all have value. The Florida climate obviously did not insure that this would happen. But it did enable people who wanted to believe it would happen so to believe.

However, speculation does not depend entirely on the capacity for self-delusion. In Florida land was divided into building lots and sold for a 10 per cent down payment. Palpably, much of the unlovely terrain that thus changed hands was as repugnant to the people who bought it as to the passer-by. The buyers did not expect to live on it; it was not easy to suppose that anyone ever would. But these were academic considerations. The reality was that this dubious asset was gaining in value by the day and could be sold at a handsome profit in a fortnight. It is another feature of the speculative mood that, as time passes, the tendency to look beyond the simple fact of increasing values to the reasons on which it depends greatly diminishes. And there is no reason why anyone should do so as long as the supply of people who buy with the expectation of selling at a profit continues to be augmented at a sufficiently rapid rate to keep prices rising.

Through 1925 the pursuit of effortless riches brought people to Florida in satisfactorily increasing numbers. More land was subdivided each week. What was loosely called seashore became five, ten, or fifteen miles from the nearest brine. Suburbs became an astonishing distance from town. As the speculation spread northward, an enterprising Bostonian, Mr. Charles Ponzi, developed a subdivision "near Jacksonville." It was approximately sixty-five miles west of the city. (In other respects Ponzi believed in good, compact neighborhoods; he sold twenty-three lots to the acre.) In instances where the subdivision was close to town, as in the case of Manhattan Estates, which were "not more than three fourths of a mile from the prosperous and fast-growing city of Nettie," the city, as was so of Nettie, did not exist. The congestion of traffic into the state became so severe that in the autumn of 1925 the railroads were forced to proclaim an embargo on less essential freight, which included building materials for developing the subdivisions. Values rose wonderfully. Within forty miles of Miami "inside" lots sold at from $8000 to $20,000; waterfront lots brought from $15,000 to $25,000, and more or less bona fide seashore sites brought $20,000 to $75,000.[4]

However, in the spring of 1926, the supply of new buyers, so essential to the reality of increasing prices, began to fail. As 1928 and 1929 were to show, the momentum built up by a good boom is not dissipated in a moment. For a while in 1926 the increasing eloquence of the promoters offset the diminishing supply of prospects. (Even the cathedral voice of William Jennings Bryan, which once had thundered against the cross of gold, had been for a time enlisted in the sorry task of selling swampland.) But this boom was not left to collapse of its own weight. In the autumn of 1926, two hurricanes showed, in the words of Frederick Lewis Allen, "what a Soothing Tropic Wind could do when it got a running start from the West Indies."[5] The worst of these winds, on September 18, 1926, killed four hundred people, tore the roofs from thousands of houses, and piled

[4] These details are principally from two articles on the Florida land boom by Homer B. Vanderblue in *The Journal of Land and Public Utility Economics,* May and August 1927.

[5] *Only Yesterday* (New York: Harper, 1931), p. 280. Other details of the damage resulting from the hurricane are from this still fresh and lively book.

tons of water and a number of elegant yachts into the streets of Miami. There was agreement that the storm had caused a healthy breathing spell in the boom, although its resumption was predicted daily. In the *Wall Street Journal* of October 8, 1926, one Peter O. Knight, an official of the Seaboard Air Line and a sincere believer in the future of Florida, acknowledged that some seventeen or eighteen thousand people were in need of assistance. But he added: "The same Florida is still there with its magnificent resources, its wonderful climate, and its geographical position. It is the Riviera of America." He expressed concern that the solicitation of Red Cross funds for hurricane relief would "do more damage permanently to Florida than would be offset by the funds received." [6]

This reluctance to concede that the end has come is also in accordance with the classic pattern. The end had come in Florida. In 1925 bank clearings in Miami were $1,066,-528,000; by 1928 they were down to $143,364,000.[7] Farmers who had sold their land at a handsome price and had condemned themselves as it later sold for double, treble, quadruple the original price, now on occasion got it back through a whole chain of subsequent defaults. Sometimes it was equipped with eloquently named streets and with sidewalks, street lamps, and taxes and assessments amounting to several times its current value.

The Florida boom was the first indication of the mood of the twenties and the conviction that God intended the American middle class to be rich. But that this mood survived the Florida collapse is still more remarkable. It was widely understood that things had gone to pieces in Florida. While the number of speculators was almost certainly small

[6] Vanderblue, *op. cit.*, p. 114.
[7] Allen, *op. cit.*, p. 282.

compared with the subsequent participation in the stock market, nearly every community contained a man who was known to have taken "quite a beating" in Florida. For a century after the collapse of the South Sea Bubble, Englishmen regarded the most reputable joint stock companies with some suspicion. Even as the Florida boom collapsed, the faith of Americans in quick, effortless enrichment in the stock market was becoming every day more evident.

III

It is hard to say when the stock market boom of the nineteen-twenties began. There were sound reasons why, during these years, the prices of common stocks should rise. Corporate earnings were good and growing. The prospect seemed benign. In the early twenties stock prices were low and yields favorable.

In the last six months of 1924, the prices of securities began to rise, and the increase was continued and extended through 1925. Thus at the end of May 1924, the *New York Times* average of the prices of twenty-five industrial stocks was 106; by the end of the year it was 134.[8] By December

[8] Throughout this book I have used the *New York Times* industrial averages as the short-hand designation of the level of security prices. This series is the arithmetical, unweighted average of the prices of twenty-five of what the *Times* describes as "good, sound stocks with regular price changes and generally active markets." The selection of the *Times* averages in preference to the Dow-Jones or other averages was largely arbitrary. The *Times* averages are the ones I have watched over the years; they are somewhat more accessible to the non-professional observer than the Dow-Jones averages. Also, while the latter are much better known, they carry in their wake a certain lore of market theory which is irrelevant for present purposes. The industrial rather than the railroad or combined average is cited because industrial stocks were the major focus of speculation and displayed the widest amplitude of movement. Unless there is indication to the contrary, values given are those at the close of the market for the date indicated.

31, 1925, it had gained very nearly another 50 points and stood at 181. The advance through 1925 was remarkably steady; there were only a couple of months when values did not show a net gain.

During 1926 there was something of a setback. Business was off a little in the early part of that year; it was thought by many that values the year before had risen unreasonably. February brought a sharp fall in the market, and March a rather abrupt collapse. The *Times* industrials went down from 181 at the beginning of the year to 172 at the end of February, and then dropped by nearly 30 points to 143 at the end of March. However, in April the market steadied and renewed its advance. Another mild setback occurred in October, just after the hurricane blew away the vestiges of the Florida boom, but again recovery was prompt. At the end of the year values were about where they had been at the beginning.

In 1927 the increase began in earnest. Day after day and month after month the price of stocks went up. The gains by later standards were not large, but they had an aspect of great reliability. Again in only two months in 1927 did the averages fail to show an increase. On May 20, when Lindbergh took off from Roosevelt Field and headed for Paris, a fair number of citizens were unaware of the event. The market, which that day was registering another of its small but solid gains, had by then acquired a faithful band of devotees who spared no attention for more celestial matters.

In the summer of 1927 Henry Ford rang down the curtain on the immortal Model T and closed his plant to prepare for Model A. The Federal Reserve index of industrial production receded, presumably as a result of the Ford shutdown, and there was general talk of depression. The effect on the market was imperceptible. At the end of the year, by which time production had also turned up again, the *Times* industrials had reached 245, a net gain of 69 points for the year.

The year 1927 is historic from another point of view in the lore of the stock market. According to a long accepted doctrine, it was in this year that the seeds of the eventual disaster were sown. The responsibility rests with an act of generous but ill-advised internationalism. Some — including Mr. Hoover — have thought it almost disloyal, although in those days accusations of treason were still made with some caution.

In 1925, under the aegis of the then Chancellor of the Exchequer, Mr. Winston Churchill, Britain returned to the gold standard at the old or pre-World War I relationship between gold, dollars, and the pound. There is no doubt that Churchill was more impressed by the grandeur of the traditional, or $4.86, pound than by the more subtle consequences of overvaluation, which he is widely assumed not to have understood. The consequences, nonetheless, were real and severe. Customers of Britain had now to use these costly pounds to buy goods at prices that still reflected wartime inflation. Britain was, accordingly, an unattractive place for foreigners to buy. For the same reason it was an easy place in which to sell. In 1925 began the long series of exchange crises which, like the lions in Trafalgar Square and the street walkers in Piccadilly, are now an established part of the British scene. There were also unpleasant domestic consequences; the bad market for coal and the effort to reduce costs and prices to meet world competition led to the general strike in 1926.

Then, as since, gold when it escaped from Britain or Europe came to the United States. This might be discouraged if prices of goods were high and interest rates were low in this country. (The United States would be a poor place in which to buy and invest.) In the spring of 1927, three august pilgrims — Montagu Norman, the Governor of the Bank of England, the durable Hjalmar Schacht, then Governor of the Reichsbank, and Charles Rist, the Deputy Governor of the Bank of France — came to the United States to urge an easy money policy. (They had previously pled with success for a roughly similar policy in 1925.) The Federal Reserve obliged. The rediscount rate of the New York Federal Reserve Bank was cut from 4 to 3.5 per cent. Government securities were purchased in considerable volume with the mathematical consequence of leaving the banks and individuals who had sold them with money to spare. Adolph C. Miller, a dissenting member of the Federal Reserve Board, subsequently described this as "the greatest and boldest operation ever undertaken by the Federal Reserve System, and . . . [it] resulted in one of the most costly errors committed by it or any other banking system in the last 75 years!" [9] The funds that the Federal Reserve made available were either invested in common stocks or (and more important) they became available to help finance the purchase of common stocks by others. So provided with funds, people rushed into the market. Perhaps the most widely read of all the interpretations of the period, that of Professor Lionel Robbins of the London School of Economics, concludes: "From that date, according to all the evidence, the situation got completely out of control." [10]

This view that the action of the Federal Reserve authori-

[9] Testimony before Senate Committee, quoted by Lionel Robbins, *The Great Depression* (New York: Macmillan, 1934), p. 53.
[10] *Ibid.*, p. 53.

ties in 1927 was responsible for the speculation and collapse which followed has never been seriously shaken. There are reasons why it is attractive. It is simple, and it exonerates both the American people and their economic system from any substantial blame. The danger of being guided by foreigners is well known, and Norman and Schacht had some special reputation for sinister motives.

Yet the explanation obviously assumes that people will always speculate if only they can get the money to finance it. Nothing could be farther from the case. There were times before and there have been long periods since when credit was plentiful and cheap — far cheaper than in 1927–29 — and when speculation was negligible. Nor, as we shall see later, was speculation out of control after 1927, except that it was beyond the reach of men who did not want in the least to control it. The explanation is a tribute only to a recurrent preference, in economic matters, for formidable nonsense.

IV

Until the beginning of 1928, even a man of conservative mind could believe that the prices of common stock were catching up with the increase in corporation earnings, the prospect for further increases, the peace and tranquility of the times, and the certainty that the Administration then firmly in power in Washington would take no more than necessary of any earnings in taxes. Early in 1928, the nature of the boom changed. The mass escape into make-believe, so much a part of the true speculative orgy, started in earnest. It was still necessary to reassure those who required some tie, however tenuous, to reality. And, as will be seen presently, this process of reassurance — of inventing the industrial equivalents of the Florida climate — eventu-

ally achieved the status of a profession. However, the time
had come, as in all periods of speculation, when men sought
not to be persuaded of the reality of things but to find
excuses for escaping into the new world of fantasy.

There were many indications by 1928 that this phase had
come. Most obvious was the behavior of the market. While
the winter months of 1928 were rather quiet, thereafter
the market began to rise, not by slow, steady steps, but by
great vaulting leaps. On occasion it also came down the
same way, only to recover and go higher again. In March
1928 the industrial average rose nearly 25 points. News of the
boiling market was frequently on the front page. Individual
issues sometimes made gains of 10, 15, and 20 points in a
single day's trading. On March 12, Radio, in many
respects the speculative symbol of the time, gained 18
points. On the following day it opened 22 points above
the previous close. Then it lost 20 points on the announcement that the behavior of the trading in the stock was being investigated by the Exchange, gained 15 points, and fell
off 9.[11] A few days later, on a strong market, it made another
18-point gain.

The March boom also celebrated, beyond anything there-
tofore, the operations of the big professional traders. The
lore of competitive markets pictures the stock exchange as
the most impersonal of markets. No doctrine is more jeal-
ously guarded by the prophets and defenders of the Stock
Exchange. "The Exchange is a market place where prices
reflect the basic law of supply and demand," the New York
Stock Exchange says firmly of itself.[12] Yet even the most
devout Wall Streeter allows himself on occasion to believe
that more personal influences have a hand in his destiny.

[11] Allen, *op. cit.*, p. 297.
[12] *Understanding the New York Stock Exchange*, 3rd ed. (New York:
Stock Exchange, April 1954), p. 2.

Somewhere around there are big men who put stocks up
and put them down.

As the boom developed, the big men became more and
more omnipotent in the popular or at least in the speculative
view. In March, according to this view, the big men decided to put the market up, and even some serious scholars
have been inclined to think that a concerted move cata-
lyzed this upsurge. If so, the important figure was John J.
Raskob. Raskob had impressive associations. He was a
director of General Motors, an ally of the Du Ponts and soon
to be Chairman of the Democratic National Committee by
choice of Al Smith. A contemporary student of the market,
Professor Charles Amos Dice of the Ohio State University,
thought this latter appointment a particular indication of the
new prestige of Wall Street and the esteem in which it was
held by the American people. "Today," he observed, "the
shrewd, worldly-wise candidate of one of the great political
parties chooses one of the outstanding operators in the
stock market . . . as a goodwill creator and popular vote
getter." [13]

On March 23, 1928, on taking ship for Europe, Raskob
spoke favorably of prospects for automobile sales for the
rest of the year and of the share in the business that General Motors would have. He may also have suggested —
the evidence is not entirely clear — that G.M. stock should
be selling at not less than twelve times earnings. This
would have meant a price of 225 as compared with a current quotation of about 187. Such, as the *Times* put it, was
"the magic of his name" that Mr. Raskob's "temperate bit
of optimism" sent the market into a boiling fury. On March
24, a Saturday, General Motors gained nearly 5 points, and
the Monday following it went to 199. The surge in Gen-

[13] *New Levels in the Stock Market* (New York: McGraw-Hill, 1929),
p. 9.

eral Motors, meanwhile, set off a great burst of trading elsewhere in the list.

Among the others who were assumed to have put their strength behind the market that spring was William Crapo Durant. Durant was the organizer of General Motors, whom Raskob and the Du Ponts had thrown out of the company in 1920. After a further adventure in the auto business, he had turned to full-time speculation in the stock market. The seven Fisher brothers were also believed to be influential. They too were General Motors alumni and had come to Wall Street with the great fortune they had realized from the sale of the Fisher-body plants. Still another was Arthur W. Cutten, the Canadian-born grain speculator who had recently shifted his market operations to Wall Street from the Chicago Board of Trade. As a market operator, Cutten surmounted substantial personal handicaps. He was very hard of hearing, and some years later, before a congressional committee, even his own counsel conceded that his memory was very defective.

Observing this group as a whole Professor Dice was especially struck by their "vision for the future and boundless hope and optimism." He noted that "they did not come into the market hampered by the heavy armor of tradition." In recounting their effect on the market, Professor Dice obviously found the English language verging on inadequacy. "Led by these mighty knights of the automobile industry, the steel industry, the radio industry . . ." he said, "and finally joined, in despair, by many professional traders who, after much sack-cloth and ashes, had caught the vision of progress, the Coolidge market had gone forward like the phalanxes of Cyrus, parasang upon parasang and again parasang upon parasang . . ." [14]

[14] *Ibid.*, pp. 6–7.

v

In June of 1928 the market retreated a parasang or two —
in fact, the losses during the first three weeks were almost
as great as the March gains. June 12, a day of particularly
heavy losses, was a landmark. For a year or more, men of
vision had been saying that the day might come when five
million shares would be traded on the New York Stock Exchange. Once this had been only a wild conversational
gambit, but for some time it had shown signs of being over-
taken by the reality. On March 12, the volume of trading
had reached 3,875,910 shares, an all-time high. By the end
of the month such a volume had become commonplace. On
March 27, 4,790,270 shares were traded. Then on June 12,
5,052, 790 shares changed hands. The ticker also fell nearly
two hours behind the market; Radio dropped 23 points, and
a New York paper began its accounts of the day's events,
"Wall Street's bull market collapsed yesterday with a deto-
nation heard round the world."

The announcement of the death of the bull market was
as premature as any since that of the death of Mark Twain.
In July there was a small net gain, and in August a strong
upsurge. Thereafter not even the approach of the election
caused serious hesitation. People remained unperturbed
when, on September 17, Roger W. Babson told an audience
in Wellesley, Massachusetts, that "if Smith should be elected
with a Democratic Congress we are almost certain to have
a resulting business depression in 1929." He also said that
"the election of Hoover and a Republican Congress should
result in continued prosperity for 1929," and it may have
been that the public knew it would be Hoover. In any case,
during the same month reassurance came from still higher
authority. Andrew W. Mellon said, "There is no cause for
worry. The high tide of prosperity will continue."

Mr. Mellon did not know. Neither did any of the other public figures who then, as since, made similar statements. These are not forecasts; it is not to be supposed that the men who make them are privileged to look farther into the future than the rest. Mr. Mellon was participating in a ritual which, in our society, is thought to be of great value for influencing the course of the business cycle. By affirming solemnly that prosperity will continue, it is believed, one can help insure that prosperity will in fact continue. Especially among businessmen the faith in the efficiency of such incantation is very great.

VI

Hoover was elected in a landslide. This, were the speculators privy to Mr. Hoover's mind, should have caused a heavy fall in the market. In his memoirs Mr. Hoover states that as early as 1925 he became concerned over the "growing tide of speculation." [15] During the months and years that followed this concern gradually changed to alarm, and then to something only slightly less than a premonition of total disaster. "There are crimes," Mr. Hoover said of speculation, "far worse than murder for which men should be reviled and punished." [16] As Secretary of Commerce he had sought nothing so much as to get the market under control.

Mr. Hoover's attitude toward the market was, however, an exceptionally well-kept secret. People did not know of his efforts, uniformly frustrated by Coolidge and the Federal Reserve Board, to translate his thoughts into action. The news of his election, so far from causing a panic, set off the greatest increase in buying to date. On November 7,

[15] *The Memoirs of Herbert Hoover: The Great Depression, 1929–1941* (New York: Macmillan, 1952), p. 5.
[16] *Ibid.*, p. 14.

the day after the election, there was a "victory boom," and the market leaders climbed 5 to 15 points. Volume reached 4,894,670 shares, or only a little less than the all-time record of June 12, and this new level was reached on a rising, not a falling market. On November 16, a further wave of buying hit the market. An astonishing 6,641,250 shares changed hands — far above the previous record. The *Times* industrial averages made a net gain of 4½ points on the day's trading — then considered an impressive advance. Apart from the afterglow of the election, there was nothing particular to incite this enthusiasm. The headlines of the day told only of the sinking of the steamship *Vestris* and the epic achievements of the officers and crew in shouldering aside the women and children and saving their own lives. November 20 was another huge day. Trading — 6,503,230 shares — was fractionally smaller than on the sixteenth, but by common agreement it was much more frantic. The following morning the *Times* observed that "for cyclonic violence yesterday's stock market has never been exceeded in the history of Wall Street."

December was not so good. Early in the month there was a bad break, and, on December 8, Radio fell a ghastly 72 points in one day. However, the market steadied and then came back. Over the whole year of 1928 the *Times* industrial average gained 86 points, or from 245 to 331. During the year Radio went from 85 to 420 (it had never paid a dividend); Du Pont went from 310 to 525; Montgomery Ward from 117 to 440; Wright Aeronautic from 69 to 289.[17] During the year 920,550,032 shares were traded on the New York Stock Exchange, as compared with a record-breaking 576,990,875 in 1927.[18] But there was still another

[17] Dice, *op. cit.*, p. 11.
[18] *Year Book, 1929–1930* (New York: Stock Exchange).

and even more significant index of what was happening
in the market. That was the phenomenal increase in trading on margin.

VII

As noted, at some point in the growth of a boom all aspects
of property ownership become irrelevant except the prospect for an early rise in price. Income from the property,
or enjoyment of its use, or even its long-run worth is now
academic. As in the case of the more repulsive Florida lots,
these usufructs may be non-existent or even negative. What
is important is that tomorrow or next week market values
will rise — as they did yesterday or last week — and a profit
can be realized.

It follows that the only reward to ownership in which the
boomtime owner has an interest is the increase in values.
Could the right to the increased value be somehow divorced
from the other and now unimportant fruits of possession
and also from as many as possible of the burdens of ownership, this would be much welcomed by the speculator. Such
an arrangement would enable him to concentrate on speculation which, after all, is the business of a speculator.

Such is the genius of capitalism that where a real demand
exists it does not go long unfilled. In all great speculative
orgies devices have appeared to enable the speculator so
to concentrate on his business. In the Florida boom the
trading was in "binders." Not the land itself but the right
to buy the land at a stated price was traded. This right
to buy — which was obtained by a down payment of 10
per cent of the purchase price — could be sold. It thus con-
ferred on the speculators the full benefit of the increase in

values. After the value of the lot had risen he could resell
the binder for what he had paid plus the full amount of
the increase in price.

The worst of the burdens of ownership, whether of land
or any other asset, is the need to put up the cash represented
by the purchase price. The use of the binder cut this burden by 90 per cent — or it multiplied tenfold the amount
of acreage from which the speculator could harvest an increase in value. The buyer happily gave up the other advantages of ownership. These included the current income
of which, invariably, there was none and the prospect of
permanent use in which he had not the slightest interest.

The stock market also has its design for concentrating
the speculative energies of the speculator, and, as might be
expected, it improves substantially on the crudities of the
real estate market. In the stock market the buyer of securities on margin gets full title to his property in an uncondi-
tional sale. But he rids himself of the most grievous burden
of ownership — that of putting up the purchase price — by
leaving his securities with his broker as collateral for the
loan that paid for them. The buyer again gets the full benefit of any increase in value — the price of the securities
goes up, but the loan that bought them does not. In the
stock market the speculative buyer also gets the earnings
of the securities he purchased. However, in the days of this
history the earnings were almost invariably less than the
interest that was paid on the loan. Often they were much
less. Yields on securities regularly ranged from nothing to
1 or 2 per cent. Interest on the loans that carried them was
often 8, 10, or more per cent. The speculator was willing to
pay to divest himself of all of the usufructs of security ownership except the chance for a capital gain.

The machinery by which Wall Street separates the oppor-

tunity to speculate from the unwanted returns and burdens
of ownership is ingenious, precise, and almost beautiful.
Banks supply funds to brokers, brokers to customers, and the
collateral goes back to banks in a smooth and all but
automatic flow. Margins — the cash which the speculator
must supply in addition to the securities to protect the
loan and which he must augment if the value of the collateral securities should fall and so lower the protection
they provide — are effortlessly calculated and watched. The
interest rate moves quickly and easily to keep the supply
of funds adjusted to the demand. Wall Street, however,
has never been able to express its pride in these arrangements. They are admirable and even wonderful only in relation to the purpose they serve. The purpose is to accommodate the speculator and facilitate speculation. But the
purposes cannot be admitted. If Wall Street confessed this
purpose, many thousands of moral men and women would
have no choice but to condemn it for nurturing an evil thing
and call for reform. Margin trading must be defended not
on the grounds that it efficiently and ingeniously assists the
speculator, but that it encourages the extra trading which
changes a thin and anemic market into a thick and healthy
one. At best this is a dull by-product and a dubious one.
Wall Street, in these matters, is like a lovely and accomplished woman who must wear black cotton stockings, heavy
woolen underwear, and parade her knowledge as a cook
because, unhappily, her supreme accomplishment is as a
harlot.

However, even the most circumspect friend of the market
would concede that the volume of brokers' loans — of loans
collateraled by the securities purchased on margin — is a
good index of the volume of speculation. Measured by this
index, the amount of speculation was rising very fast in

1928. Early in the twenties the volume of brokers' loans —
because of their liquidity they are often referred to as
call loans or loans in the call market — varied from a billion
to a billion and a half dollars. By early 1926 they had increased to two and a half billions and remained at about
that level for most of the year. During 1927 there was another increase of about a billion dollars, and at the end of
the year they reached $3,480,780,000. This was an incred-
ible sum, but it was only the beginning. In the two dull
winter months of 1928 there was a small decline and then
expansion began in earnest. Brokers' loans reached four
billion on the first of June 1928, five billion on the first of
November, and by the end of the year they were well along
to six billion.[19] Never had there been anything like it before.

People were swarming to buy stocks on margin — in other
words, to have the increase in price without the costs of
ownership. This cost was being assumed, in the first instance, by the New York banks, but they, in turn, were
rapidly becoming the agents for lenders the country over
and even the world around. There is no mystery as to why
so many wished to lend so much in New York. One of the
paradoxes of speculation in securities is that the loans that
underwrite it are among the safest of all investments. They
are protected by stocks which under all ordinary circumstances are instantly salable, and by a cash margin as well.
The money, as noted, can be retrieved on demand. At the
beginning of 1928 this admirably liquid and exceptionally
secure outlet for non-risk capital was paying around 5 per
cent. While 5 per cent is an excellent gilt-edged return,
the rate rose steadily through 1928, and during the last week

[19] The year-end figure was $5,722,258,724. Figures are from the New
York Stock Exchange *Year Book, 1928–1929*, and do not include brokers'
time loans.

of the year it reached 12 per cent. This was still with complete safety.

In Montreal, London, Shanghai, and Hong Kong there was talk of these rates. Everywhere men of means told themselves that 12 per cent was 12 per cent. A great river of gold began to converge on Wall Street, all of it to help Americans hold common stock on margin. Corporations also found these rates attractive. At 12 per cent Wall Street might even provide a more profitable use for the working capital of a company than additional production. A few firms made this decision: instead of trying to produce goods with its manifold headaches and inconveniences, they confined themselves to financing speculation. Many more companies started lending their surplus funds on Wall Street.

There were still better ways of making money. In principle, New York banks could borrow money from the Federal Reserve Bank for 5 per cent and re-lend it in the call market for 12. In practice they did. This was, possibly, the most profitable arbitrage operation of all time.

VIII

However, there were many ways of making money in 1928. Never had there been a better time to get rich, and people knew it. 1928, indeed, was the last year in which Americans were buoyant, uninhibited, and utterly happy. It wasn't that 1928 was too good to last; it was only that it didn't last.

In the January issue of *World's Work*, Will Payne, after reflecting on the wonders of the yea · just over, went on to explain the difference between a gambler and an investor. A gambler, he pointed out, wins only because someone else loses. Where it is investment all gain. One investor, he explained, buys General Motors at $100, sells it to another at $150, who sells it to a third at $200. Everyone makes money. As Walter Bagehot once observed: "All people are most credulous when they are most happy." [20]

[20] *Lombard Street*, 1922 ed. (London: John Murray, 1922), p. 151.

CHAPTER II

Something Should Be Done?

PURELY IN RETROSPECT it is easy to see how 1929 was destined to be a year to remember. This was not because Mr. Hoover was soon to become President and had inimical intentions toward the market. Those intentions developed at least partly in retrospect. Nor was it because men of wisdom could tell that a depression was overdue. No one, wise or unwise, knew or now knows when depressions are due or overdue.

Rather, it was simply that a roaring boom was in progress in the stock market and, like all booms, it had to end. On the first of January of 1929, as a simple matter of probability, it was most likely that the boom would end before the year was out, with a diminishing chance that it would end in any given year thereafter. When prices stopped rising — when the supply of people who were buying for an increase was exhausted — then ownership on margin would become meaningless and everyone would want to sell. The market wouldn't level out; it would fall precipitately.

All this being so, the position of the people who had at least nominal responsibility for what was going on was a complex one. One of the oldest puzzles of politics is who is to regulate the regulators. But an equally baffling problem, which has never received the attention it deserves, is who is to make wise those who are required to have wisdom.

Some of those in positions of authority wanted the boom

to continue. They were making money out of it, and they may have had an intimation of the personal disaster which awaited them when the boom came to an end. But there were also some who saw, however dimly, that a wild speculation was in progress and that something should be done. For these people, however, every proposal to act raised the same intractable problem. The consequences of successful action seemed almost as terrible as the consequences of inaction, and they could be more horrible for those who took the action.

A bubble can easily be punctured. But to incise it with a needle so that it subsides gradually is a task of no small delicacy. Among those who sensed what was happening in early 1929, there was some hope but no confidence that the boom could be made to subside. The real choice was between an immediate and deliberately engineered collapse and a more serious disaster later on. Someone would certainly be blamed for the ultimate collapse when it came. There was no question whatever as to who would be blamed should the boom be deliberately deflated. (For nearly a decade the Federal Reserve authorities had been denying their responsibility for the deflation of 1920–21.) The eventual disaster also had the inestimable advantage of allowing a few more days, weeks, or months of life. One may doubt if at any time in early 1929 the problem was ever framed in terms of quite such stark alternatives. But however disguised or evaded, these were the choices which haunted every serious conference on what to do about the market.

II

The men who had responsibility for these ineluctable choices were the President of the United States, the Secretary of the

Treasury, the Federal Reserve Board in Washington, and the Governor and Directors of the Federal Reserve Bank of New York. As the most powerful of the Federal Reserve Banks, and the one with the market at its doorstep, the New York bank both had and assumed responsibilities which were not accepted by the other eleven banks of the system.

President Coolidge neither knew nor cared what was going on. A few days before leaving office in 1929, he cheerily observed that things were "absolutely sound" and that stocks were "cheap at current prices." [1] In earlier years, whenever warned that speculation was getting out of hand, he had comforted himself with the thought that this was the primary responsibility of the Federal Reserve Board.[2] The Board was a semi-autonomous body precisely because Congress wanted to protect it from excessive political interference by the Executive.

However tender his scruples, President Coolidge could have acted through his Secretary of the Treasury, who served, ex-officio, as a member of the Federal Reserve Board. The Secretary also had the primary responsibility for economic and especially for financial policy. But on this as on other matters of economic policy, the incumbent, Andrew W. Mellon, was a passionate advocate of inaction. The responsibility thus passed to the Federal Reserve Board and the Federal Reserve Banks.

The regulation of economic activity is without doubt the most inelegant and unrewarding of public endeavors. Almost everyone is opposed to it in principle; its justification always relies on the unprepossessing case for the lesser evil. Regulation originates in raucous debate in Congress in which the

[1] *The Memoirs of Herbert Hoover*, p. 16.
[2] *Ibid.*, p. 11.

naked interests of pressure groups may at times involve an exposure bordering on the obscene. Promulgation and enforcement of rules and regulations is by grinding bureaucracies which are ceaselessly buffeted by criticism. In recent times it has become obligatory for the regulators at every opportunity to confess their inadequacy, which in any case is all too evident.

The great exception to this dreary story is the regulatory activity of the central bank — with us, the Federal Reserve System. Here is regulation of a seemly and becoming sort. No one apologizes for it; men of impeccable conservatism would rise to espouse such regulation were they called upon to do so, which they almost never are. This regulation is not the work of thousands of clerks, statisticians, hearing officers, lawyers, and lesser beings in a teeming office building on the Mall. Rather it emerges in the measured and orderly discussion of men of quiet and dignified mien, each at his accustomed place around a handsome table in a richly paneled and richly draperied room. These men do not issue orders; at most they suggest. Chiefly they move interest rates, buy or sell securities and, in doing so, nudge the economy here and restrain it there. Because the meanings of their actions are not understood by the great majority of the people, they can reasonably be assumed to have superior wisdom. Their actions will on occasion be criticized. More often they will be scrutinized for hidden meaning.

Such is the *mystique* of central banking. Such was the awe-inspiring role in 1929 of the Federal Reserve Board in Washington, the policy-making body which guided and directed the twelve Federal Reserve banks. However, there was a jarring difficulty. The Federal Reserve Board in those times was a body of startling incompetence.

For several years, until late in 1927, the Chairman and

guiding genius presumptive, was one Daniel R. Crissinger. He had been trained for his task by serving as General Counsel of the Marion Steam Shovel Company of Marion, Ohio. There is no indication that he was an apt student. However, his background seemed satisfactory to another Marion boy, Warren G. Harding, who had brought him to Washington, where he was regarded as a hack politician from Ohio. In 1927 Crissinger was replaced by Roy A. Young, who for eight years had been Governor of the Minneapolis Federal Reserve Bank. Young, a more substantial figure, was undoubtedly aware of what was going on. However, he was a man of caution who sought no fame as a martyr to the broken boom. His colleagues were among the more commonplace of Harding-Coolidge appointees. With one exception — the erstwhile college professor, Adolph C. Miller — they have been conservatively described by Herbert Hoover as "mediocrities." [3]

The New York Federal Reserve Bank was under more vigorous leadership. For several years, until 1928, its governor had been Benjamin Strong, the first American since Nicholas Biddle to make an important reputation as a central banker. Strong's views were regarded throughout the System with only little less awe than the gold standard. However, in the view of Herbert Hoover — and in this instance Hoover's views are widely shared — Strong, so far from being concerned about the inflation, was the man most responsible for it. It was he who took the lead in 1927 in easing money rates to help the hard-pressed Europeans. For this Mr. Hoover later called him "a mental annex to Europe." [4]

This is unfair. Governor Strong's action was entirely reason-

[3] *Ibid.*, p. 9.
[4] *Ibid.*, p. 9, 10.

able in the circumstances and, as noted in the last chapter, it takes more to start a speculation than a general ability to borrow money. Still, the New York Federal Reserve Bank, under Governor Strong's leadership may not have been sufficiently perturbed by the speculation a block or two away. Nor was it after Governor Strong died in October 1928 and was replaced by George L. Harrison. A reason, no doubt, was the reassurance provided by people in high places who were themselves speculating heavily. One such was Charles E. Mitchell, the Chairman of the Board of the National City Bank who, on January 1, 1929, became a class A director of the Federal Reserve Bank of New York. The end of the boom would mean the end of Mitchell. He was not a man to expedite his own demise.

III

In the accepted history of these times, the Federal Reserve authorities are held to be not so much unaware or unwilling as impotent. They would have liked to stop the boom, but they lacked the means. This puts far too elaborate a face on matters. And it largely disguises the real nature of the dilemma which the authorities faced.

The classic instruments of control were indeed largely useless. These, as almost every college sophomore knows, are two: open market operations and the manipulation of the rediscount rate. Open market sales of government securities [5] by the Federal Reserve bring to the vaults of the Reserve Banks the cash which is paid for the securities. There it remains sterile and harmless. Had it stayed in the commercial banks it would have been loaned to the public in multiple volume and particularly in those days to people who were buying common stocks.

[5] Or the sale or reduction in inventory of commercial paper.

If such a policy is to succeed, the Federal Reserve System rather obviously must have securities to sell. One of the inestimable blessings of the years of depression, war, and deficit-financing since 1930 is a spacious inventory of government debt in the Reserve Banks. In 1929 the Banks were not so well endowed. At the beginning of 1928, holdings were $617 million. During the first half of the year there were heavy sales as part of an effort to dry up the supply of funds that was feeding the market. Although sales were discontinued in the latter part of the year in the highly erroneous belief that the policy had succeeded and that the boom was under control, they couldn't have been continued much longer in any case. By the end of 1928 the inventory of government securities of the Federal Reserve System amounted to only $228 million. Had these all been dropped into the market, they might possibly have had some effect. But the Board was not given to any such drastic behavior which, incidentally, would also have largely denuded the Reserve Banks of earning assets. Sales were made a few millions at a time in the early months of 1929, but the effect was inconsequential. Moreover, even in following this feeble policy the Board worried lest, in denying funds to the stock market, it might put a pinch on "legitimate" business. The Reserve Banks continued to buy acceptances — the security that emerges in the course of financing ordinary non-speculative trade — and, relieved of the need to carry this paper, the commercial banks happily loaned more money in the stock market.

The other instrument of Federal Reserve policy was the rediscount rate. This is the rate at which member commercial banks borrow from the Reserve Banks of their district so that they may accommodate more borrowers than their own resources permit. In January 1929, the rediscount rate at the New York Federal Reserve Bank was 5 per cent. The rate on brokers' loans ranged from 6 to 12 per cent. Only a drastic increase would have made it unprofitable for a bank to borrow at the Federal Reserve in order to lend the proceeds, directly or indirectly, in the stock market. Apart from the general aversion to drastic action, such an increase would also have raised rates to ordinary businessmen, consumers, and farmers. In fact, higher interest rates would have been distressing to everyone but the speculator. A man who paid, say, an average of 10 per cent to carry his holdings of Radio through 1928 would not have been either deterred or much disturbed had the rate been twice that high. During the same year, he made 500 per cent on the appreciation in the value of his investment.

On February 14, 1929, the New York Federal Reserve Bank proposed that the rediscount rate be raised from 5 to 6 per cent to check speculation. The Federal Reserve Board in Washington thought this a meaningless gesture which would only increase rates to business borrowers. A long controversy ensued in which President Hoover sided with the Board against the Bank. The rate was not increased until late in the summer.

There was another circumstance which gave the Reserve authorities an admirable excuse for inaction. That was the previously noted flow of funds from corporations and individuals to the market. During 1929, Standard Oil of New Jersey contributed a daily average of $69 million to the call market; Electric Bond and Share averaged over $100 million.[6] A few corporations — Cities Service was one — even sold securities and loaned the proceeds in the stock market.[7] By early 1929, loans from these non-banking sources were approximately equal to those from the banks. Later they became much

[6] *Stock Exchange Practices*, Report of the Committee on Banking and Currency pursuant to Senate Resolution 84 (Washington, 1934), p. 16.
[7] *Ibid.*, pp. 13–14.

greater. The Federal Reserve authorities took for granted
that they had no influence whatever over this supply of
funds.

IV

In fact, the Federal Reserve was helpless only because it
wanted to be. Had it been determined to do something, it
could for example have asked Congress for authority to halt
trading on margin by granting the Board the power to set
margin requirements. Margins were not low in 1929; a
residue of caution had caused most brokers to require customers to put up in cash 45 to 50 per cent of the value of
the stocks they were buying. However, this was all the cash
numerous of their customers had. An increase in margins to,
say, 75 per cent in January 1929, or even a serious proposal to
do so, would have caused many small speculators and quite a
few big ones to sell. The boom would have come to a sudden
and perhaps spectacular end. (The power to fix margin requirements was eventually given to the Federal Reserve
Board by the Securities Exchange Act in 1934, a year in
which the danger of a revival of speculation about equaled
that of a renascence of prohibition.)

Actually, not even new legislation, or the threat of it, was
needed. In 1929, a robust denunciation of speculators and
speculation by someone in high authority and a warning that
the market was too high would almost certainly have broken
the spell. It would have brought some people back from
the world of make-believe. Those who were planning to
stay in the market as long as possible but still get out (or go
short) in time would have got out or gone short. Their occu-
pational nervousness could readily have been translated into
an acute desire to sell. Once the selling started, some more
vigorously voiced pessimism could easily have kept it going.

The very effectiveness of such a measure was the problem. Of all the weapons in the Federal Reserve arsenal, words were the most unpredictable in their consequences. Their effect might be sudden and terrible. Moreover, these consequences could be attributed with the greatest of precision to the person or persons who uttered the words. Retribution would follow. To the more cautious of the Federal Reserve officials in the early part of 1929 silence seemed literally golden.

Yet the boom was continuing. In January the *Times* industrials gained 30 points, more than during the post-election spree in November. Brokers' loans went up a whopping $260 million; on five different days, three of them as the market got off to a boiling start right after New Year's, trading on the New York Stock Exchange exceeded the magic five-million mark. Effective action would be disastrous; yet some action seemed unavoidable. Finally the Board decided to write a letter and issue a press release. It could do no less.

On February 2, it addressed the individual Reserve Banks as follows:

> A member [commercial bank] is not within its reasonable claims for re-discount facilities at its reserve bank when it borrows either for the purpose of making speculative loans or for the purpose of maintaining speculative loans. The board has no disposition to assume authority to interfere with the loan practices of member banks, so long as they do not involve the Federal reserve banks. It has, however, a grave responsibility whenever there is evidence that member banks are maintaining speculative security loans with the aid of Federal reserve credit.[8]

On February 7, in what may be an even finer example of

[8] Thomas Wilson, *Fluctuations in Income and Employment*, p. 147.

fiduciary prose — connoisseurs will wish to read it backward as well as forward — the Board warned the public:

> When [the Board] finds that conditions are arising which obstruct the Federal reserve banks in the effective discharge of their functions of so managing the credit facilities of the Federal reserve system as to accommodate commerce and business, it is its duty to inquire into them and to take such measures as may be deemed suitable and effective in the circumstances to correct them; which, in the immediate situation, means to restrain the use, either directly or indirectly, of Federal Reserve facilities in aid of the growth of speculative credit.[9]

Almost simultaneously with this warning came the news that the Bank of England was raising the bank rate from 4½ to 5½ per cent in an effort to diminish the flow of British funds to the new Golconda. The result was a sharp break in the market. On February 7, in a five-million share day, the *Times* industrials dropped 11 points, with a further drop on the day following. Thereafter the market recovered, but, for February as a whole, there was no appreciable net gain. Economists have long had a phrase for this action — it was called the Federal Reserve's effort at "moral suasion." Since the market was only temporarily checked, there has been ever since virtually complete agreement that moral suasion was a failure.

Precisely the opposite conclusion could and probably should have been drawn. It is impossible to imagine a milder, more tentative, more palpably panic-stricken communiqué than that issued by the Board. The statement that the Board had no intention of interfering with loans to support speculation so long as Federal Reserve credit was not

9 *Ibid.*, pp. 147–48.

involved is especially noteworthy. Clearly the Federal Reserve was less interested in checking speculation than in detaching itself from responsibility for the speculation that was going on. And it will be observed that some anonymous draftsman achieved a wording which indicated that not the present level but only a further growth in speculation would be viewed with alarm. Yet in the then state of nervousness even these almost incredibly feeble words caused a sharp setback.

v

The nervousness of the market and the unsuspected moral authority of the equally nervous men of the Federal Reserve was even better illustrated in March. As the new month approached, Mr. Coolidge made his blithe observation about stocks being cheap and the country being sound. The market surged up in what the papers dubbed "The Inaugural Market," and on March 4, his attitude toward speculators still unknown, Mr. Hoover took over. The market for the next couple of weeks remained strong.

Then toward the end of the month disquieting news reached Wall Street. The Federal Reserve Board was meeting daily in Washington. It issued no statements. Newspapermen pressed the members after the sessions and were met with what then, as now, was known as tight-lipped silence. There was not a hint as to what the meetings were about, although everyone knew they concerned the market. The meetings continued day after day, and there was also an unprecedented Saturday session.

Soon it was too much. On Monday, March 25, the first market day following the unseemly Saturday meeting, the tension became unbearable. Although, or rather because,

Washington was still silent, people began to sell. Speculative favorites — Commercial Solvents, Wright Aero, American Railway Express — dropped 10 or 12 points or more; the *Times* industrial average was off 9½ points for the day. More important, some banks decided that, in the event of a Federal Reserve crackdown, virtue might have a reward above revenue. They began curtailing their loans in the call market, and the rate on brokers' loans went to 14 per cent.

On the next day, Tuesday, March 26, everything was much worse. The Federal Reserve Board was still maintaining its by now demoralizing silence. A wave of fear swept the market. More people decided to sell, and they sold in astonishing volume. An amazing 8,246,740 shares changed hands on the New York Stock Exchange, far above any previous record. Prices seemed to drop vertically. At the low for the day 20- and 30-point losses were commonplace. The *Times* industrials at one time were 15 points below the previous day's close. Thousands of speculators, in whose previous experience the market had always risen, now saw for the first time the seamy side of their new way of life. Each new quotation was far below the last one. Moreover, the ticker, unable to cope with the unprecedented volume, was far behind the market. Not only were things bad, but they had almost certainly become worse, yet one couldn't tell from the ticker how much worse. Before the day was out many of these thousands received a peremptory telegram from their brokers — a telegram that was in the starkest of contrast with the encouraging, half-confidential, rich-uncle tone of all previous communications. It asked more margin promptly.

Meanwhile the banks continued to trim sails for the storm. It is probable that some professional traders were selling because they foresaw the moment when there would be no money with which to carry stocks on margin. And that moment might be near, for on the morning of March 26, the rate on call money reached 20 per cent, its high for the 1929 boom.

March 26, 1929, could have been the end. Money could have remained tight. The authorities might have remained firm in their intention to keep it so. The panic might have continued. Each fall in prices would have forced a new echelon of speculators to sell, and so forced prices down still more. It did not happen, and if any man can be credited with this, the credit belongs to Charles E. Mitchell. The Federal Reserve authorities were ambivalent, but Mitchell was not. He was for the boom. Moreover, his prestige as head of one of the two largest and most influential commercial banks, his reputation as an aggressive and highly successful investment banker, and his position as a director of the New York Federal Reserve Bank meant that he spoke with at least as much authority as anyone in Washington. During the day, as money tightened, rates rose, and the market fell, Mitchell decided to take a hand. He told the press, "We feel that we have an obligation which is paramount to any Federal Reserve warning, or anything else, to avert any dangerous crisis in the money market." The National City, he said, would loan money as necessary to prevent liquidation. It would also (and did) borrow from the New York Federal Reserve Bank to do what the Federal Reserve Board had warned against doing. Disguised only slightly by the prose form of finance, Mitchell issued the Wall Street counterpart of Mayor Hague's famous manifesto, "I am the law in Jersey City."

Mitchell's words were like magic. By the end of trading on the 26th money rates had eased, and the market had rallied. The Federal Reserve remained silent, but now its silence was reassuring. It meant that it conceded Mitchell's mastery. The next day the National City regularized its commitment to the boom: it announced that it would insure reasonable interest rates by putting $25 million into the call market — $5 million when the rate was 16 per cent, and $5 million additional for each percentage point. In its monthly letter a few days later, the bank justified its position and, incidentally, gave an admirable statement of the dilemma which the Federal Reserve faced. (The National City was in no doubt which horn of the dilemma it preferred.) The letter said: "The National City Bank fully recognizes the dangers of overspeculation [sic] and endorses the desire of the Federal Reserve authorities to restrain excessive credit expansion for this purpose. At the same time, the bank, business generally, and it may be assumed the Federal Reserve Banks . . . wish to avoid a general collapse of the securities markets such as would have a disastrous effect on business." [10]

VI

Mitchell did not escape criticism. A Senate investigation was mentioned. Senator Carter Glass, who as the sponsor of the Federal Reserve legislation had a keen proprietary interest in its operation, said: "He avows his superior obligation to a frantic stock market over against the obligation of his oath as a director of the New York Federal Reserve Bank . . . the Bank should ask for [his] immediate resignation." That the Federal Reserve Board never dreamed of doing any such thing may be taken as a further indication

[10] Quoted by Mitchell in *Stock Exchange Practices*, Hearings, Subcommittee, Senate Committee on Banking and Currency — The Pecora Committee, February–March 1933, Pt. 6, p. 1817.

that its moral suasion was being administered with a very infirm touch.

And the Federal Reserve was criticized even more than Mitchell — even though it could hardly have done less than it did. Arthur Brisbane said judiciously: "If buying and selling stocks is wrong the government should close the Stock Exchange. If not, the Federal Reserve should mind its own business." In a leading article in *Barron's,* a Mr. Seth Axley was less even-handed: "For the Federal Reserve Board to deny investors the means of recognizing economies which are now proved, skill which is now learned, and inventions which are almost unbelievable seems to justify doubt whether it is adequately interpreting the times." [11] Since the principal action which the Federal Reserve had taken against investors had been to hold meetings and maintain silence, this was doubtless a trifle harsh. However, it was positively kind as compared with the words of a young Princeton scholar who emerged at this time as a leading defender of Wall Street.

Joseph Stagg Lawrence's book *Wall Street and Washington,* when it appeared later in the year bearing the distinguished imprimatur of the Princeton University Press, was described by a leading financial journal as a "breath of fresh air." The regulatory concern of the Federal Reserve about Wall Street, Mr. Lawrence said in this remarkable volume, was motivated strictly by bias — a bias "founded upon a clash of interests and a moral and intellectual antipathy between the wealthy, cultured, and conservative settlements on the seacoast [including Wall Street] and the poverty stricken, illiterate, and radical pioneer communities of the interior." [12] The cultured and conservative Mr. Lawrence

[11] *Barron's,* May 6, 1929.
[12] *Wall Street and Washington* (Princeton: Princeton University Press, 1929), p. 3.

also had hard words for the defenders of the Federal Reserve in the Senate, including, oddly enough, the seacoast senator from Virginia, Carter Glass. "It seems incredible that in the year of our Grace 1929 a body of presumably intelligent public men should permit fanatical passions and provincial ignorance to find expression in unrestrained virulence. Yet this is precisely what has taken place . . . When the Senator from the Old Dominion rose in that chamber of absurdities, sometimes referred to as a deliberative assembly, his remarks were characterized by neither reason nor restraint. Blatant bigotry and turbulent provincialism have joined to condemn an innocent community." [13] Some hardened Wall Streeters may have been surprised when they realized that the "innocent community" meant them.

VII

After the defeat by Mitchell in March, the Federal Reserve retired from the field. There continued to be some slight anxiety as to what it might do. In April, William Crapo Durant is supposed to have paid a secret night visit to the White House to warn President Hoover that if the Board were not called off it would precipitate a terrible crash. The President was noncommittal, and Durant is said to have reduced his holdings before leaving on a trip to Europe.[14] In June from Princeton Mr. Lawrence said that the Board was still "doing its utmost to cast the proverbial monkey wrench into the machinery of prosperity." He warned the Board that it had "aroused the enmity of an honest, intelligent, and

13 *Ibid.*, p. v.
14 The visit is described by Earl Sparling, *Mystery Men of Wall Street* (New York: Greenberg, 1930), pp. 3–8. The authority is dubious, although the author's facts, as distinct from his interpretation, are frequently accurate.

public-spirited community." [15] (This also was Wall Street.) But the Board, in fact, had decided to leave that honest, intelligent, and public-spirited community strictly to its own devices. It realized, Governor Young said subsequently, that "while the hysteria might be somewhat restrained," it would have to run its course, and the Reserve Banks could only brace themselves for the "inevitable collapse." [16] More accurately, the Federal Reserve authorities had decided not to be responsible for the collapse.

In August the Board finally agreed to an increase in the rediscount rate to 6 per cent. The market weakened only for a day. Any conceivable consequence of the action was nullified by a simultaneous easing of the buying rate on acceptances.

In fact, from the end of March on, the market had nothing further to fear from authority. President Hoover did ask Henry M. Robinson, a Los Angeles banker, to proceed as his emissary to New York and talk to the bankers there about the boom. According to Mr. Hoover, Robinson was assured that things were sound. [17] Richard Whitney, the Vice-President of the Exchange, was also summoned to the White House and told that something should be done about speculation. Nothing was done, and Mr. Hoover was able to find some solace in the thought that primary responsibility for regulating the stock exchange rested with the Governor of New York, Franklin D. Roosevelt. [18]

[15] *Barron's,* June 10, 1929.
[16] Seymour E. Harris, *Twenty Years of Federal Reserve Policy* (Cambridge: Harvard University Press, 1933), p. 547. I have made much use of this ultra-conservative but very careful account of Federal Reserve policy.
[17] Hoover, *Memoirs,* p. 17.
[18] *Ibid.* Mr. Hoover, who is careless of such details, including his dates, describes Whitney as President of the Exchange, which he only later became.

Roosevelt, too, was following a laissez-faire policy, at least on the matter of the stock market. A firm of investment counselors in Boston, called McNeel's Financial Service, describing itself with a deft Back Bay touch as "An Aristocracy of Successful Investors," advertised a new guide to investment. The headline read: "He made $70,000 after reading *Beating the Stock Market*." No doubt whoever it was did. He might have made it without reading the volume or without being able to read. For now, free at last from all threat of government reaction or retribution, the market sailed off into the wild blue yonder. Especially after June 1 all hesitation disappeared. Never before or since have so many become so wondrously, so effortlessly, and so quickly rich. Perhaps Messrs. Hoover and Mellon, and the Federal Reserve were right in keeping their hands off. Perhaps it was worth being poor for a long time to be so rich for just a little while.

CHAPTER III

In Goldman, Sachs We Trust

THE RECONDITE PROBLEMS of Federal Reserve policy were not the only questions that were agitating Wall Street intellectuals in the early months of 1929. There was worry that the country might be running out of common stocks. One reason prices of stocks were so high, it was explained, was that there weren't enough to go around, and, accordingly, they had acquired a "scarcity value." Some issues, it was said, were becoming so desirable that they would soon be taken out of the market and would not reappear at any price.

If, indeed, common stocks were becoming scarce it was in spite of as extraordinary a response of supply to demand as any in the history of that well-worn relationship. Without doubt, the most striking feature of the financial era which ended in the autumn of 1929 was the desire of people to buy securities and the effect of this on values. But the increase in the number of securities to buy was hardly less striking. And the ingenuity and zeal with which companies were devised in which securities might be sold was as remarkable as anything.

Not all of the increase in the volume of securities in 1928 and 1929 was for the sole purpose of accommodating the speculator. It was a good time to raise money for general corporate purposes. Investors would supply capital with enthusiasm and without tedious questions. (Seaboard Air Line was a speculative favorite of the period in part because

many supposed it to be an aviation stock with growth possibilities.) In these years of prosperity men with a vision of
still greater prosperity stretching on and on and forever,
naturally saw the importance of being well provided with
plant and working capital. This was no time to be niggardly.

Also, it was an age of consolidation, and each new merger
required, inevitably, some new capital and a new issue of
securities to pay for it. A word must be said about the
merger movement of the twenties.

It was not the first such movement but, in many respects,
it was the first of its kind. Just before and just after the turn
of the century in industry after industry, small companies
were combined into large ones. The United States Steel
Corporation, International Harvester, International Nickel,
American Tobacco, and numerous other of the great corporations trace to this period. In these cases the firms which were
combined produced the same or related products for the same
national market. The primary motivation in all but the rarest
cases was to reduce, eliminate, or regularize competition.
Each of the new giants dominated an industry, and henceforth exercised measurable control over prices and production, and perhaps also over investment and the rate of tech-
nological innovation.

A few such mergers occurred in the twenties. Mostly, however, the mergers of this period brought together not firms in
competition with each other but firms doing the same thing
in different communities. Local electric, gas, water, bus, and
milk companies were united in great regional or national systems. The purpose was not to eliminate competition, but
rather the incompetence, somnambulance, naïveté, or even
the unwarranted integrity of local managements. In the
twenties, a man in downtown New York or Chicago could
take unabashed pride in the fact that he was a financial

genius. The local owners and managers were not. There was no false modesty when it came to citing the advantages of displacing yokels with a central management of decent sophistication.

In the case of utilities the instrument for accomplishing this centralization of management and control was the holding company. These bought control of the operating companies. On occasion they bought control of other holding companies which controlled yet other holding companies, which in turn, directly or indirectly through yet other holding companies, controlled the operating companies. Everywhere local power, gas, and water companies passed into the possession of a holding-company system.

Food retailing, variety stores, department stores, and motion picture theatres showed a similar, although not precisely identical, development. Here, too, local ownership gave way to central direction and control. The instrument of this centralization, however, was not the holding company but the corporate chain. These, more often than not, instead of taking over existing businesses, established new outlets.

The holding companies issued securities in order to buy operating properties, and the chains issued securities in order to build new stores and theatres. While in the years before 1929 the burgeoning utility systems — Associated Gas and Electric, Commonwealth and Southern, and the Insull companies — attracted great attention, the chains were at least as symbolic of the era. Montgomery Ward was one of the prime speculative favorites of the period; it owed its eminence to the fact that it was a chain and thus had a particularly bright future. The same was true of Woolworth, American Stores, and others. Interest in branch and chain banking was also strong, and it was widely felt that state and federal laws were an archaic barrier to a consolidation which would knit the small-town and small-city banks into a few regional and national systems. Various arrangements for defeating the intent of the law, most notably bank holding companies, were highly regarded.

Inevitably promoters organized some new companies merely to capitalize on the public interest in industries with a new and wide horizon and provide securities to sell. Radio and aviation stocks were believed to have a particularly satisfactory prospect, and companies were formed which never had more than a prospect. In September 1929, an advertisement in the *Times* called attention to the impending arrival of television and said with considerable prescience that the "commercial possibilities of this new art defy imagination." The ad opined, somewhat less presciently, that sets would be in use in homes that fall. However, in the main, the market boom of 1929 was rooted directly or indirectly in existing industries and enterprises. New and fanciful issues for new and fanciful purposes, ordinarily so important in times of speculation, played a relatively small part. No significant amount of stock was sold in companies "To make Salt Water Fresh — For building of Hospitals for Bastard Children — For building of Ships against Pirates — For importing a Number of large Jack Asses from Spain," or even "For a Wheel of Perpetual Motion," to cite a representative list of promotions at the time of the South Sea Bubble.[1]

II

The most notable piece of speculative architecture of the late twenties, and the one by which, more than any other device, the public demand for common stocks was satisfied, was the investment trust or company. The investment trust

[1] Walter Bagehot, *Lombard Street*, pp. 130, 131.

did not promote new enterprises or enlarge old ones. It merely arranged that people could own stock in old companies through the medium of new ones. Even in the United States, in the twenties, there were limits to the amount of real capital which existing enterprises could use or new ones could be created to employ. The virtue of the investment trust was that it brought about an almost complete divorce of the volume of corporate securities outstanding from the volume of corporate assets in existence. The former could be twice, thrice, or any multiple of the latter. The volume of underwriting business and of securities available for trading on the exchanges all expanded accordingly. So did the securities to own, for the investment trusts sold more securities than they bought. The difference went into the call market, real estate, or the pockets of the promoters. It is hard to imagine an invention better suited to the time or one better designed to eliminate the anxiety about the possible shortage of common stocks.

The idea of the investment trust is an old one, although, oddly enough, it came late to the United States. Since the eighteen-eighties in England and Scotland, investors, mostly smaller ones, had pooled their resources by buying stock in an investment company. The latter, in turn, invested the funds so secured. A typical trust held securities in from five hundred to a thousand operating companies. As a result, the man with a few pounds, or even a few hundred, was able to spread his risk far more widely than were he himself to invest. And the management of the trusts could be expected to have a far better knowledge of companies and prospects in Singapore, Madras, Capetown, and the Argentine, places to which British funds regularly found their way, than the widow in Bristol or the doctor in Glasgow. The smaller risk and better information well justified the modest compensation of those who managed the enterprise. Despite some early misadventures, the investment trusts soon became an established part of the British scene.

Before 1921 in the United States only a few small companies existed for the primary purpose of investing in the securities of other companies.[2] In that year, interest in investment trusts began to develop, partly as the result of a number of newspaper and magazine articles describing the English and Scottish trusts. The United States, it was pointed out, had not been keeping abreast of the times; other countries were excelling us in fiduciary innovation. Soon, however, we began to catch up. More trusts were organized, and by the beginning of 1927 an estimated 160 were in existence. Another 140 were formed during that year.[3]

The managers of the British trusts normally enjoy the greatest of discretion in investing the funds placed at their disposal. At first the American promoters were wary of asking for such a vote of confidence. Many of the early trusts were trusts — the investor bought an interest in a specified assortment of securities which were then deposited with a trust company. At the least the promoters committed themselves to a rigorous set of rules on the kinds of securities to be purchased and the way they were to be held and managed. But as the twenties wore along, such niceties disappeared. The investment trust became, in fact, an investment corporation.[4] It sold its securities to the public — sometimes just common stock, more often common and preferred

[2] One estimate puts the number at about forty. Cf. *Investment Trusts and Investment Companies*, Pt. I, Report of the Securities and Exchange Commission (Washington, 1939), p. 36.

[3] *Ibid.*, p. 36.

[4] And would be more accurately described as an investment company or investment corporation. However, I have kept here to the less precise but more customary usage.

stock, debenture and mortgage bonds — and the proceeds were then invested as the management saw fit. Any possible tendency of the common stockholder to interfere with the management was prevented by selling him non-voting stock or having him assign his voting rights to a management-controlled voting trust.

For a long time the New York Stock Exchange looked with suspicion on the investment trusts; only in 1929 was listing permitted. Even then the Committee on the Stock List required an investment trust to post with the Exchange the book and market value of the securities held at the time of listing and once a year thereafter to provide an inventory of its holdings. This provision confined the listing of most of the investment trusts to the Curb, Boston, Chicago, or other road company exchanges. Apart from its convenience, this refusal to disclose holdings was thought to be a sensible precaution. Confidence in the investment judgment of the managers of the trusts was very high. To reveal the stocks they were selecting might, it was said, set off a dangerous boom in the securities they favored. Historians have told with wonder of one of the promotions at the time of the South Sea Bubble. It was "For an Undertaking which shall in due time be revealed." The stock is said to have sold exceedingly well. As promotions the investment trusts were, on the record, more wonderful. They were undertakings the nature of which was never to be revealed, and their stock also sold exceedingly well.

III

During 1928 an estimated 186 investment trusts were organized; by the early months of 1929 they were being promoted at the rate of approximately one each business day, and a total of 265 made their appearance during the course of the year. In 1927 the trusts sold to the public about $400,000,000 worth of securities; in 1929 they marketed an estimated three billions worth. This was at least a third of all the new capital issues in that year; by the autumn of 1929 the total assets of the investment trusts were estimated to exceed eight billions of dollars. They had increased approximately elevenfold since the beginning of 1927.[5]

The parthenogenesis of an investment trust differed from that of an ordinary corporation. In nearly all cases it was sponsored by another company, and by 1929 a surprising number of different kinds of concerns were bringing the trusts into being. Investment banking houses, commercial banks, brokerage firms, securities dealers, and, most important, other investment trusts were busy giving birth to new trusts. The sponsors ranged in dignity from the House of Morgan, sponsor of the United and Alleghany Corporations, down to one Chauncey D. Parker, the head of a fiscally perilous investment banking firm in Boston, who organized three investment trusts in 1929 and sold $25,000,000 worth of securities to an eager public. Chauncey then lost most of the proceeds and lapsed into bankruptcy.[6]

Sponsorship of a trust was not without its rewards. The sponsoring firm normally executed a management contract with its offspring. Under the usual terms, the sponsor ran the investment trust, invested its funds, and received a fee based on a percentage of capital or earnings. Were the sponsor a stock exchange firm, it also received commissions on the purchase and sale of securities for its trust. Many of the sponsors were investment banking firms, which meant, in effect,

[5] The estimates in this paragraph are all from *Investment Trusts and Investment Companies*, Pt. III, Chap. 1, pp. 3, 4.

[6] *Ibid.*, Pt. III, Chap. 2, p. 37 ff.

that the firm was manufacturing securities it could then bring
to market. This was an excellent way of insuring an adequate
supply of business.

The enthusiasm with which the public sought to buy investment trust securities brought the greatest rewards of all.
Almost invariably people were willing to pay a sizable premium over the offering price. The sponsoring firm (or *its* promoters) received allotments of stock or warrants which en-
titled them to stock at the offering price. These they were
then able to sell at once at a profit. Thus one of the enterprises of the Mr. Chauncey D. Parker just mentioned — a
company with the resounding name of Seaboard Utilities
Shares Corporation — issued 1,600,000 shares of common
stock on which the company netted $10.32 a share. That,
however, was not the price paid by the public. It was the
price at which the stock was issued to Parker and his colleagues. They in turn sold their shares to the public at from
$11 to $18.25 and split the profit with the dealers who
marketed the securities.[7]

Operations of this sort were not confined to the lowly or
the vaguely disreputable. J. P. Morgan and Company, which
(with Bonbright and Company) sponsored United Corporation in January 1929, offered a package of one share of common stock and one of preferred to a list of friends, Morgan
partners included, at $75. This was a bargain. When trading
in United Corporation began a week later, the price was 92
bid, 94 asked on the over-the-counter market, and after four
days the stock reached 99. Stock that had been taken up at
75 could be and was promptly resold at these prices.[8] That
such agreeable incentives greatly stimulated the organization
of new investment trusts is hardly surprising.

[7] *Ibid.*, p. 39.
[8] *Stock Exchange Practices.* Report (Washington, 1934), pp. 103–4.

IV

There were some, indeed, who only regretted that everyone could not participate in the gains from these new engines of financial progress. One of those who had benefited from the United Corporation promotion just mentioned was John J. Raskob. As Chairman of the Democratic National Committee, he was also politically committed to a firm friendship for the people. He believed that everyone should be in on the kind of opportunities he himself enjoyed.

One of the fruits of this generous impulse during the year was an article in the *Ladies' Home Journal* with the attractive title, "Everybody Ought to be Rich." In it Mr. Raskob pointed out that anyone who saved fifteen dollars a month, invested it in sound common stocks, and spent no dividends would be worth — as it then appeared — some eighty thousand dollars after twenty years. Obviously, at this rate, a great many people could be rich.

But there was the twenty-year delay. Twenty years seemed a long time to get rich, especially in 1929, and for a Democrat and friend of the people to commit himself to such gradualism was to risk being thought a reactionary. Mr. Raskob, therefore, had a further suggestion. He proposed an investment trust which would be specifically designed to allow the poor man to increase his capital just as the rich man was doing.

The plan, which Mr. Raskob released to the public in the early summer of 1929, was worked out in some detail. (The author stated that he had discussed it with "financiers, economists, theorists, professors, bankers, labor leaders, industrial leaders, and many men of no prominence who have ideas.") A company would be organized to buy stocks. The proletarian with, say, $200 would turn over his pittance to the company which would then buy stocks in the rather less meager amount of $500. The additional $300 the company would get from a financial subsidiary organized for the purpose, and with which it would post all of the stock as collateral. The incipient capitalist would pay off his debt at the rate of perhaps $25 a month. He would, of course, get the full benefit of the increase in the value of the stock, and this was something that Mr. Raskob regarded as inevitable. Hammering home the inadequacy of existing arrangements, Mr. Raskob said: "Now all the man with $200 to $500 to invest can do today is to buy Liberty bonds . . ." [9]

The reaction to the Raskob plan was comparable to the response to a new and daring formulation of the relation of mass to energy. "A practical Utopia," one paper called it. Another described it as "The greatest vision of Wall Street's greatest mind." A tired and cynical commentator was moved to say that it looks "more like financial statesmanship than anything that has come out of Wall Street in many a weary moon." [10]

Had there been a little more time, it seems certain that something would have been made of Mr. Raskob's plan. People were full of enthusiasm for the wisdom and perspicacity of such men. This was admirably indicated by the willingness of people to pay for the genius of the professional financier.

v

The measure of this respect for financial genius was the relation of the market value of the outstanding securities of the investment trusts to the value of the securities it owned. Normally the securities of the trust were worth considerably

[9] *The Literary Digest*, June 1, 1929.
[10] *Ibid.*

more than the property it owned. Sometimes they were worth twice as much. There should be no ambiguity on this point. The only property of the investment trust was the common and preferred stocks and debentures, mortgages, bonds, and cash that it owned. (Often it had neither office nor office furniture; the sponsoring firm ran the investment trust out of its own quarters.) Yet, had these securities all been sold on the market, the proceeds would invariably have been less, and often much less, than the current value of the outstanding securities of the investment company. The latter, obviously, had some claim to value which went well beyond the assets behind them.

That premium was, in effect, the value an admiring community placed on professional financial knowledge, skill, and manipulative ability. To value a portfolio of stocks "at the market" was to regard it only as inert property. But as the property of an investment trust it was much more, for the portfolio was then combined with the precious ingredient of financial genius. Such special ability could invoke a whole strategy for increasing the value of securities. It could join in pools and syndicates to put up values. It knew when others were doing likewise and could go along. Above all, the financial genius was in on things. It had access to what Mr. Lawrence of Princeton described as "the stage whereon is focused the world's most intelligent and best informed judgment of the values of the enterprises which serve men's needs." [11] One might make money investing directly in Radio, J. I. Case, or Montgomery Ward, but how much safer and wiser to let it be accomplished by the men of peculiar knowledge, and wisdom.

By 1929 the investment trusts were aware of their reputation for omniscience, as well as its importance, and they lost

[11] *Wall Street and Washington,* p. 163.

no opportunity to enlarge it. To have a private economist was one possibility, and as the months passed a considerable competition developed for those men of adequate reputation and susceptibility. It was a golden age for professors. The American Founders Group, an awe-inspiring family of investment trusts, had as a director Professor Edwin W. Kemmerer, the famous Princeton money expert. The staff economist was Dr. Rufus Tucker, also a well-known figure. (That economists were not yet functioning with perfect foresight is perhaps suggested by the subsequent history of the enterprise. United Founders, the largest company in the group, suffered a net contraction in its assets of $301,385,504 by the end of 1935, and its stock dropped from a high of over $75 share in 1929 to a little under 75 cents.)[12]

Still another great combine was advised by Dr. David Friday, who had come to Wall Street from the University of Michigan. Friday's reputation for both insight and foresight was breathtaking. A Michigan trust had three college professors — Irving Fisher of Yale, Joseph S. Davis of Stanford, and Edmund E. Day then of Michigan — to advise on its policies.[13] The company stressed not only the diversity of its portfolio but also of its counsel. It was fully protected from any parochial Yale, Stanford, or Michigan view of the market.

Other trusts urged the excellence of their genius in other terms. Thus one observed that, since it owned stocks in 120 corporations, it benefited from the "combined efficiency of their presidents, officers, and the boards of directors." It noted further that "closely allied to these corporations are the great banking institutions." Then, in something of a logical

[12] Bernard J. Reis, *False Security* (New York: Equinox, 1937), pp. 117 ff. and 296.
[13] *Investment Trusts and Investment Companies*, Pt. I, p. 111.

broad jump, it concluded, "The trust, therefore, mobilizes to a large extent the successful business intellect of the country." Another concern, less skilled in logical method, contented itself with pointing out that "Investing is a science instead of a 'one-man job.'" [14]

As 1929 wore along, it was plain that more and more of the new investors in the market were relying on the intellect and the science of the trusts. This meant, of course, that they still had the formidable problem of deciding between the good and the bad trusts. That there were some bad ones was (though barely) recognized. Writing in the March 1929 issue of *The Atlantic Monthly*, Paul C. Cabot stated that dishonesty, inattention, inability, and greed were among the common shortcomings of the new industry. These were impressive disadvantages, and as an organizer and officer of a promising investment trust, the State Street Investment Corporation, Mr. Cabot presumably spoke with some authority.[15] However, audience response to such warnings in 1929 was very poor. And the warnings were very infrequent.

VI

Knowledge, manipulative skill, or financial genius were not the only magic of the investment trust. There was also leverage. By the summer of 1929, one no longer spoke of investment trusts as such. One referred to high-leverage trusts, low-leverage trusts, or trusts without any leverage at all.

The principle of leverage is the same for an investment trust as in the game of crack-the-whip. By the application of well-known physical laws, a modest movement near the point of origin is translated into a major jolt on the extreme

[14] *Ibid.*, Pt. I, pp. 61, 62.
[15] *Ibid.*, Pt. III, Ch. I, p. 53.

periphery. In an investment trust leverage was achieved by issuing bonds, preferred stock, as well as common stock to purchase, more or less exclusively, a portfolio of common stocks. When the common stock so purchased rose in value, a tendency which was always assumed, the value of the bonds and preferred stock of the trust was largely unaffected.[16] These securities had a fixed value derived from a specified return. Most or all of the gain from rising portfolio values was concentrated on the common stock of the investment trust which, as a result, rose marvelously.

Consider, by way of illustration, the case of an investment trust organized in early 1929 with a capital of $150 million — a plausible size by then. Let it be assumed, further, that a third of the capital was realized from the sale of bonds, a third from preferred stock, and the rest from the sale of common stock. If this $150 million were invested, and if the securities so purchased showed a normal appreciation, the portfolio value would have increased by midsummer by about 50 per cent. The assets would be worth $225 million. The bonds and preferred stock would still be worth only $100 million; their earnings would not have increased, and they could claim no greater share of the assets in the hypothetical event of a liquidation of the company. The remaining $125 million, therefore, would underlie the value of the common stock of the trust. The latter, in other words, would have increased in asset value from $50 million to $125 million, or by 150 per cent, and as the result of an increase of only 50 per cent in the value of the assets of the trust as a whole.

This was the magic of leverage, but this was not all of it. Were the common stock of the trust, which had so miracu-

16 Assuming they were reasonably orthodox. Bonds and preferred stock, in these days, were issues with an almost infinite variety of conversion and participation rights.

lously increased in value, held by still another trust with similar leverage, the common stock of *that* trust would get an increase of between 700 and 800 per cent from the original 50 per cent advance. And so forth. In 1929 the discovery of the wonders of the geometric series struck Wall Street with a force comparable to the invention of the wheel. There was a rush to sponsor investment trusts which would sponsor investment trusts, which would, in turn, sponsor investment trusts. The miracle of leverage, moreover, made this a relatively costless operation to the ultimate man behind all of the trusts. Having launched one trust and retained a share of the common stock, the capital gains from leverage made it relatively easy to swing a second and larger one which enhanced the gains and made possible a third and still bigger trust.

Thus, Harrison Williams, one of the more ardent exponents of leverage, was thought by the Securities and Exchange Commission to have substantial influence over a combined investment trust and holding company system with a market value in 1929 at close to a billion dollars.[17] This had been built on his original control of a smallish concern — the Central States Electric Corporation — which was worth only some six million dollars in 1921.[18] Leverage was also a prime factor in the remarkable growth of the American Founders Group. The original member of this notable family of investment trusts was launched in 1921. The original promoter was, unhappily, unable to get the enterprise off the ground

[17] Part of it shared with Goldman, Sachs, as will be noted presently. The line between a holding company, which has investment in and control of an operating company (or another holding company), and an investment trust or company, which has investment but which is presumed not to have control, is often a shadowy one. The pyramiding of holding companies and concomitant leverage effects was also a striking feature of the period.

[18] *Investment Trusts and Investment Companies*, Pt. III, Ch. 1, pp. 5, 6

because he was in bankruptcy. However, the following year a friend contributed $500, with which modest capital a second trust was launched, and the two companies began business. The public reception was highly favorable, and by 1927 the two original companies and a third which had subsequently been added had sold between seventy and eighty million dollars worth of securities to the public.[19] But this was only the beginning; in 1928 and 1929 an explosion of activity struck the Founders Group. Stock was sold to the public at a furious rate. New firms with new names were organized to sell still more stock until, by the end of 1929, there were thirteen companies in the group.

At that time the largest company, the United Founders Corporation, had total resources of $686,165,000. The group as a whole had resources with a market value of more than a billion dollars, which may well have been the largest volume of assets ever controlled by an original outlay of $500. Of the billion dollars, some $320,000,000 was represented by inter-company holdings — the investment of one or another company of the group in the securities of yet others. This fiscal incest was the instrument through which control was maintained and leverage enjoyed. Thanks to this long chain of holdings by one company in another, the increases in values in 1928 and 1929 were effectively concentrated in the value of the common stock of the original companies.

Leverage, it was later to develop, works both ways. Not all of the securities held by the Founders were of a kind calculated to rise indefinitely, much less to resist depression. Some years later the portfolio was found to have contained 5000 shares of Kreuger and Toll, 20,000 shares of Kolo Products Corporation, an adventuresome new company which was

[19] *Ibid.*, Pt. I, pp. 98–100.

to make soap out of banana oil, and $295,000 in the bonds of the Kingdom of Yugoslavia.[20] As Kreuger and Toll moved down to its ultimate value of nothing, leverage was also at work — geometric series are equally dramatic in reverse. But this aspect of the mathematics of leverage was still un-revealed in early 1929, and notice must first be taken of the most dramatic of all the investment company promotions of that remarkable year, those of Goldman, Sachs.

VII

Goldman, Sachs and Company, an investment banking and brokerage partnership, came rather late to the investment trust business. Not until December 4, 1928, less than a year before the stock market crash, did it sponsor the Goldman Sachs Trading Corporation, its initial venture in the field. However, rarely, if ever, in history has an enterprise grown as the Goldman Sachs Trading Corporation and its offspring grew in the months ahead.

The initial issue of stock in the Trading Corporation was a million shares, all of which was bought by Goldman, Sachs and Company at $100 a share for a total of $100,000,000. Ninety per cent was then sold to the public at $104. There were no bonds and no preferred stocks; leverage had not yet been discovered by Goldman, Sachs and Company. Control of the Goldman Sachs Trading Corporation remained with Goldman, Sachs and Company by virtue of a management contract and the presence of the partners of the company on the board of the Trading Corporation.[21]

In the two months after its formation, the new company sold some more stock to the public, and on February 21 it

[20] Reis, *op. cit.*, p. 124.
[21] *Stock Exchange Practices*, Hearings, April–June 1932, Pt. 2, pp. 566, 567.

merged with another investment trust, the Financial and Industrial Securities Corporation. The assets of the resulting company were valued at $235 million, reflecting a gain of well over 100 per cent in under three months. By February 2, roughly three weeks before the merger, the stock for which the original investors had paid $104 was selling for $136.50. Five days later, on February 7, it reached $222.50. At this latter figure it had a value approximately twice that of the current total worth of the securities, cash, and other assets owned by the Trading Corporation.

This remarkable premium was not the undiluted result of public enthusiasm for the financial genius of Goldman, Sachs. Goldman, Sachs had considerable enthusiasm for itself, and the Trading Corporation was buying heavily of its own securities. By March 14 it had bought 560,724 shares of its own stock for a total outlay of $57,021,936.[22] This, in turn, had boomed their value. However, perhaps foreseeing the exiguous character of an investment company which had its investments all in its own common stock, the Trading Corporation stopped buying itself in March. Then it resold part of the stock to William Crapo Durant, who re-resold it to the public as opportunity allowed.

The spring and early summer were relatively quiet for Goldman, Sachs, but it was a period of preparation. By July 26 it was ready. On that date the Trading Corporation, jointly with Harrison Williams, launched the Shenandoah Corporation, the first of two remarkable trusts. The initial securities issue by Shenandoah was $102,500,000 (there was an additional issue a couple of months later) and it was reported to have been oversubscribed some sevenfold. There were both preferred and common stock, for by now Goldman,

[22] Details here are from *Investment Trusts and Investment Companies*, Pt. III, Ch. 1, pp. 6 ff. and 17 ff.

Sachs knew the advantages of leverage. Of the five million shares of common stock in the initial offering, two million were taken by the Trading Corporation, and two million by Central States Electric Corporation on behalf of the co-sponsor, Harrison Williams. Williams was a member of the small board along with partners in Goldman, Sachs. Another board member was a prominent New York attorney whose lack of discrimination in this instance may perhaps be attributed to youthful optimism. It was Mr. John Foster Dulles. The stock of Shenandoah was issued at $17.50. There was brisk trading on a "when issued" basis. It opened at 30, reached a high of 36, and closed at 36, or 18.5 above the issue price. (By the end of the year the price was 8 and a fraction. It later touched fifty cents.)

Meanwhile Goldman, Sachs was already preparing its second tribute to the countryside of Thomas Jefferson, the prophet of small and simple enterprises. This was the even mightier Blue Ridge Corporation, which made its appearance on August 20. Blue Ridge had a capital of $142,000,000, and nothing about it was more remarkable than the fact that it was sponsored by Shenandoah, its precursor by precisely twenty-five days. Blue Ridge had the same board of directors as Shenandoah, including the still optimistic Mr. Dulles, and of its 7,250,000 shares of common stock (there was also a substantial issue of preferred) Shenandoah sub-scribed a total of 6,250,000. Goldman, Sachs by now was applying leverage with a vengeance.

An interesting feature of Blue Ridge was the opportunity it offered the investor to divest himself of routine securities in direct exchange for the preferred and common stock of the new corporation. A holder of American Telephone and Telegraph Company could receive 4⁷⁹⁄₁₆ shares each of Blue Ridge Preference and Common for each share of Telephone stock turned in. The same privilege was extended to holders of Allied Chemical and Dye, Santa Fe, Eastman Kodak, General Electric, Standard Oil of New Jersey, and some fifteen other stocks. There was much interest in this offer.

August 20, the birthday of Blue Ridge, was a Tuesday, but there was more work to be done by Goldman, Sachs that week. On Thursday, the Goldman Sachs Trading Corporation announced the acquisition of the Pacific American Associates, a West Coast investment trust which, in turn, had recently bought a number of smaller investment trusts and which owned the American Trust Company, a large commercial bank with numerous branches throughout California. Pacific American had a capital of around a hundred million. In preparation for the merger, the Trading Corporation had issued another $71,400,000 in stock which it had exchanged for capital stock of the American Company, the holding company which owned over 99 per cent of the common stock of the American Trust Company.[23]

Having issued more than a quarter of a billion dollars worth of securities in less than a month — an operation that would not then have been unimpressive for the United States Treasury — activity at Goldman, Sachs subsided somewhat. Its members had not been the only busy people during this time. It was a poor day in August and September of that year when no new trust was announced or no large new issue of securities was offered by an old one. Thus, on August first, the papers announced the formation of Anglo-American Shares, Inc., a company which, with a *soigné* touch not often seen in a Delaware corporation, had among its directors the Marquess of Carisbrooke, GCB, GCVO, and Colonel, the

[23] Details on Shenandoah, Blue Ridge, and the Pacific American merger not from the *New York Times* of the period are from *Investment Trusts and Investment Companies*, Pt. III, Ch. 1, pp. 5–7.

Master of Sempill, AFC, otherwise identified as the President of the Royal Aeronautical Society, London. American Insuranstocks Corporation was launched the same day, though boasting no more glamorous a director than William Gibbs McAdoo. On succeeding days came Gude Winmill Trading Corporation, National Republic Investment Trust, Insull Utility Investments, Inc., International Carriers, Ltd., Tri-Continental Allied Corporation, and Solvay American Investment Corporation. On August 13 the papers also announced that an Assistant U.S. Attorney had visited the offices of the Cosmopolitan Fiscal Corporation and also an investment service called the Financial Counselor. In both cases the principals were absent. The offices of the Financial Counselor were equipped with a peephole like a speakeasy.

More investment trust securities were offered in September of 1929 even than in August — the total was above $600 million.[24] However, the nearly simultaneous promotion of Shenandoah and Blue Ridge was to stand as the pinnacle of new era finance. It is difficult not to marvel at the imagination which was implicit in this gargantuan insanity. If there must be madness something may be said for having it on a heroic scale.

Years later, on a gray dawn in Washington, the following colloquy occurred before a committee of the United States Senate.[25]

Senator Couzens. Did Goldman, Sachs and Company organize
    the Goldman Sachs Trading Corporation?
Mr. Sachs. Yes, sir.

[24] E. H. H. Simmons, *The Principal Causes of the Stock Market Crisis of Nineteen Twenty-Nine* (address issued in pamphlet form by the New York Stock Exchange, January 1930), p. 16.
[25] *Stock Exchange Practices*, Hearings, April–June 1932, Pt. 2, pp. 566–67.

Senator Couzens. And it sold its stock to the public?

Mr. Sachs. A portion of it. The firm invested originally in 10 per cent of the entire issue for the sum of $10,000,000.

Senator Couzens. And the other 90 per cent was sold to the public?

Mr. Sachs. Yes, sir.

Senator Couzens. At what price?

Mr. Sachs. At 104. That is the old stock . . . the stock was split two for one.

Senator Couzens. And what is the price of the stock now?

Mr. Sachs. Approximately 1¾.

CHAPTER IV

The Twilight of Illusion

THERE WAS no summer lull in Wall Street that year. Along with the great investment trust promotions went the greatest market ever. Every day prices rose; they almost never fell. During June the *Times* industrials went up 52 points; in July they gained another 25. This was a total gain of 77 points in two months. In all of the remarkable year of 1928 they had gone up only 86.5 points. Then in August they rose another 33 points. This gain of 110 points in three months — from 339 on the last day of May to 449 on the last day of August — meant that during the summer values had increased, over-all, by nearly a quarter.

Individual issues had also done very well. During the three summer months, Westinghouse went from 151 to 286 for a net gain of 135. General Electric was up from 268 to 391, and Steel from 165 to 258. Even so somber a security as American Tel and Tel had gone from 209 to 303. The investment trusts were making good gains. United Founders went from 36 bid to 68; Alleghany Corporation rose from 33 to 56.

The volume of trading was also consistently heavy. On the New York Stock Exchange it was frequently between four and five million shares. Only occasionally on a full day did it drop below three million. However, trading on the New York Stock Exchange was no longer a good index of the total interest in securities speculation. Many new and exciting issues — Shenandoah, Blue Ridge, Pennroad, Insull Utilities — were not listed on the Big Board. The New York Stock Exchange in those days was not a snobbish, prying, or an intolerant institution. Most companies that so desired could have their stocks listed. Nevertheless, there were some who found it wise, and many more who found it convenient not to answer the fairly elementary requests which were made by the Exchange for information. The new stocks, accordingly, were traded on the Curb, or in Boston, or on other out-of-town exchanges. Although business on the New York Stock Exchange remained larger than that on all other markets combined, its relative position suffered. (In 1929 it had an estimated 61 per cent of all transactions; three years later, when most of the new trusts had disappeared forever, the Exchange had 76 per cent of the total business.)[1] It follows that by the summer of 1929 the normally somnambulant markets of Boston, San Francisco, and even of Cincinnati were having a boom. Instead of being merely a pale reflection of the real thing on Wall Street, they had a life and personality of their own. Stocks were for sale here that couldn't be had in New York, and some of them had an exceptional speculative kick. By 1929 it was a poor town, sadly devoid of civic spirit, which wasn't wondering if it too shouldn't have a stock market.

More than the prices of common stocks were rising. So, at an appalling rate, was the volume of speculation. Brokers' loans during the summer increased at a rate of about $400,-000,000 a month. By the end of the summer, the total exceeded seven billions. Of that more than half was being supplied by corporations and individuals, at home and abroad, who were taking advantage of the excellent rate of

[1] Estimates are from *Stock Exchange Practices*, Report (Washington, 1934), p. 8.

return which New York was providing on money. Only rarely did the rate on call loans during that summer get as low as six per cent. The normal range was seven to twelve. On one occasion the rate touched fifteen. Since, as earlier observed, these loans provided all but total safety, liquidity, and ease of administration, the interest would not have seemed unattractive to a usurious moneylender in Bombay. To a few alarmed observers it seemed as though Wall Street were by way of devouring all the money of the entire world. However, in accordance with the cultural practice, as the summer passed, the sound and responsible spokesmen decried not the increase in brokers' loans, but those who insisted on attaching significance to this trend. There was a sharp criticism of the prophets of doom.

II

There were two sources of intelligence on brokers' loans. One was the monthly tabulation of the New York Stock Exchange, which in general is used here. The other was the slightly less complete return of the Federal Reserve System which was published weekly. Each Friday this report showed a large increase in loans; each Friday it was firmly stated that it didn't mean a thing, and anyone who suggested otherwise was administered a stern rebuke. It seems probable that only a minority of the people in the market related the volume of the brokers' loans to the volume of purchases on nargin and thence to the amount of speculation. Accordingly, an expression of concern over these loans was easily attacked as a gratuitous effort to undermine confidence. Thus, in *Barron's* on July 8, Sheldon Sinclair Wells explained that those who worried about brokers' loans, and about the influx of funds from corporations, simply did not know what was going on. The call market had become a great new investment outlet for corporate reserves, he argued. The critics did not appreciate this change.

Chairman Mitchell of the National City Bank, by nature an equable man, was repeatedly angered by the attention being given to brokers' loans and expressed himself strongly. The financial press was also disturbed, and when Arthur Brisbane later in the year questioned the propriety of a 10 per cent call rate, *The Wall Street Journal* reached the end of its patience. "Even in general newspapers some accurate knowledge is required for discussing most things. Why is it that any ignoramus can talk about Wall Street?" [2] (It does seem possible that Brisbane thought the rate was 10 per cent a day rather than a year.)

Scholars also reacted against those who, deliberately or otherwise, were sabotaging prosperity with their unguarded pessimism. After soberly viewing the situation, Professor Dice concluded that the high level of brokers' loans should not be "as greatly feared as some would have us believe." [3] In August the Midland Bank of Cleveland made public the results of calculations which proved that until loans by corporations in the stock market reached twelve billion there was no cause for concern. [4]

The best reassurance on brokers' loans was in the outlook for the market. If stocks remained high and went higher, and if they did so because their prospects justified their price, then there was no occasion to worry about the loans that were piling up. Accordingly, much of the defense of the loans consisted in defending the levels of the market. It was not hard to persuade people that the market was

[2] *The Wall Street Journal*, September 19, 1929.
[3] *New Levels in the Stock Market*, p. 183.
[4] *New York Times*, August 2, 1929.

sound; as always in such times they asked only that the disturbing voices of doubt be muted and that there be tolerably frequent expressions of confidence.

In 1929 treason had not yet become a casual term of reproach. As a result, pessimism was not openly equated with efforts to destroy the American way of life. Yet it had such connotations. Almost without exception, those who expressed concern said subsequently that they did so with fear and trepidation. (Later in the year a Boston firm of investment counselors struck a modern note with a widely publicized warning that America had no place for "destructionists.")

The official optimists were many and articulate. Thus in June, Bernard Baruch told Bruce Barton, in a famous interview published in *The American Magazine* [5] that "the economic condition of the world seems on the verge of a great forward movement." He pointed out that no bears had houses on Fifth Avenue. Numerous college professors also exuded scientific confidence. In light of later developments, the record of the Ivy League was especially unfortunate. In a statement which achieved minor notoriety, Lawrence of Princeton said that "the consensus of judgment of the millions whose valuations function on that admirable market, the Stock Exchange, is that stocks are not at present over-valued." He added: "Where is that group of men with the all-embracing wisdom which will entitle them to veto the judgment of this intelligent multitude?" [6]

That autumn Professor Irving Fisher of Yale made his immortal estimate: "Stock prices have reached what looks like a permanently high plateau." Irving Fisher was the most original of American economists. Happily there are better things

[5] *The American Mazagine,* June 1929.
[6] *Wall Street and Washington,* p. 179. These passages were later quoted editorially by the *New York Times* and are reproduced in turn from there.

— his contributions to index numbers, technical economic theory, and monetary theory — for which he is remembered.

From Cambridge slightly less spacious reassurance came from the Harvard Economic Society, an extracurricular enterprise conducted by a number of economics professors of unexceptionable conservatism. The purpose of the Society was to help businessmen and speculators foretell the future. Forecasts were made several times a month and undoubtedly gained in stature from their association with the august name of the university.

By wisdom or good luck, the Society in early 1929 was mildly bearish. Its forecasters had happened to decide that a recession (though assuredly not a depression) was overdue. Week by week they foretold a slight setback in business. When, by the summer of 1929, the setback had not appeared, at least in any very visible form, the Society gave up and confessed error. Business, it decided, might be good after all. This, as such things are judged, was still a creditable record, but then came the crash. The Society remained persuaded that no serious depression was in prospect. In November it said firmly that "a severe depression like that of 1920–21 is outside the range of probability. We are not facing protracted liquidation." This view the Society reiterated until it was liquidated.

III

The bankers were also a source of encouragement to those who wished to believe in the permanence of the boom. A great many of them abandoned their historic role as the guardians of the nation's fiscal pessimism and enjoyed a brief respite of optimism. They had reasons for doing so. In the years preceding, a considerable number of the commercial

72 · The Great Crash

banks, including the largest of the New York houses, had organized securities affiliates. These affiliates sold stocks and bonds to the public, and this business had become important. It was a business that compelled a rosy view of the future. In addition, individual bankers, perhaps taking a cue from the heads of the National City and Chase in New York, were speculating vigorously on their own behalf. They were unlikely to say, much less to advocate, anything that would jar the market.

However, there were exceptions. One was Paul M. Warburg of the International Acceptance Bank, whose predictions must be accorded the same prominence as the forecasts of Irving Fisher. They were remarkably prescient. In March of 1929, he called for a stronger Federal Reserve policy and argued that if the present orgy of "unrestrained speculation" were not brought promptly to a halt there would ultimately be a disastrous collapse. This, he suggested, would be unfortunate not alone for the speculators. It would "bring about a general depression involving the entire country." [7]

Only Wall Street spokesmen who took the most charitable view of Warburg contented themselves with describing him as obsolete. One said he was "sandbagging American prosperity." Others hinted that he had a motive — presumably a short position. As the market went up and up, his warnings were recalled only with contempt. [8]

The most notable skeptics were provided by the press. They were a great minority to be sure. Most magazines and most newspapers in 1929 reported the upward sweep of the market with admiration and awe and without alarm. They viewed both the present and the future with exuberance.

[7] The Commercial and Financial Chronicle, March 9, 1929, p. 1444.
[8] Alexander Dana Noyes, The Market Place (Boston: Little, Brown, 1938), p. 324.

Moreover, by 1929 numerous journalists were sternly resisting the more subtle blandishments and flattery to which they have been thought susceptible. Instead they were demanding cold cash for news favorable to the market. A financial columnist of the *Daily News,* who signed himself "The Trader," received some $19,000 in 1929 and early 1930 from a free-lance operator named John J. Levenson. "The Trader" repeatedly spoke well of stocks in which Mr. Levenson was interested. Mr. Levenson later insisted, however, that this was a coincidence and that the payment reflected his more or less habitual generosity.[9] A radio commentator named William J. McMahon was the president of the McMahon Institute of Economic Research, an organization that was mostly McMahon. He told in his broadcasts of the brilliant prospects of stocks which pool operators were seeking to boom. For this, it later developed, he received an honorarium of $250 a week from a certain David M. Lion.[10] Mr. Lion was one of several whom the Pecora Committee reported as making a business of buying favorable comment in the necessary amount at the proper moment.

At the other extreme was the best of the financial press. The established financial services like Poor's and that of the Standard Statistics Company never lost touch with reality. In the autumn Poor's *Weekly Business and Investment Letter* went so far as to speak of the "great common-stock delusion."[11] The editor of *The Commercial and Financial Chronicle* was never quite shaken in his conviction that Wall Street had taken leave of its senses. The weekly reports on the brokers' loans were regularly the occasion for a solemn warning; the news columns featured any available bad news. However, by far the greatest force for sobriety was the *New*

[9] *Stock Exchange Practices,* Hearings, April–June 1932, Pt. 2, pp. 601 ff.
[10] *Ibid.,* p. 676 ff.
[11] Quoted by Allen, *Only Yesterday,* p. 322.

York Times. Under the guidance of the veteran Alexander Dana Noyes, its financial page was all but immune to the blandishments of the New Era. A regular reader could not doubt that a day of reckoning was expected. Also, on several occasions it reported, much too prematurely, that the day of reckoning had arrived.

Indeed the temporary breaks in the market which preceded the crash were a serious trial for those who had declined fantasy. Early in 1928, in June, in December, and in February and March of 1929 it seemed that the end had come. On various of these occasions the *Times* happily reported the return to reality. And then the market took flight again. Only a durable sense of doom could survive such discouragement. The time was coming when the optimists would reap a rich harvest of discredit. But it has long since been forgotten that for many months those who resisted reassurance were similarly, if less permanently, discredited. To say that the *Times,* when the real crash came, reported the event with jubilation would be an exaggeration. Nevertheless, it covered it with an unmistakable absence of sorrow.

IV

By the summer of 1929 the market not only dominated the news. It also dominated the culture. That *recherché* minority which at other times has acknowledged its interest in Saint Thomas Aquinas, Proust, psychoanalysis, and psychosomatic medicine then spoke of United Corporation, United Founders, and Steel. Only the most aggressive of the eccentrics maintained their detachment from the market and their interest in autosuggestion or communism. Main Street had always had one citizen who could speak knowingly about buying or selling stocks. Now he became an oracle. In New

York, on the edge of any gathering of significantly interesting people there had long been a literate broker or investment counselor who was abreast of current plans for pools, syndicates, and mergers, and was aware of attractive possibilities. He helpfully advised his friends on investments, and pressed, he would always tell what he knew of the market and much that he didn't. Now these men, even in the company of artists, playwrights, poets, and beautiful concubines, suddenly shone forth. Their words, more or less literally, became golden. Their audience listened not with the casual heed of people who are collecting quotable epigrams, but with the truly rapt attention of those who expect to make money by what they hear.

That much of what was repeated about the market — then as now — bore no relation to reality is important, but not remarkable. Between human beings there is a type of intercourse which proceeds not from knowledge, or even from lack of knowledge, but from failure to know what isn't known. This was true of much of the discourse on the market. At luncheon in downtown Scranton, the knowledgeable physician spoke of the impending split-up in the stock of Western Utility Investors and the effect on prices. Neither the doctor nor his listeners knew why there should be a split-up, why it should increase values, or even why Western Utility Investors should have any value. But neither the doctor nor his audience knew that he did not know. Wisdom, itself, is often an abstraction associated not with fact or reality but with the man who asserts it and the manner of its assertion.

Perhaps the failure to visualize the extent of one's innocence was especially true of women investors, who by now were entering the market in increasing numbers. (An article in *The North American Review* in April reported that women had become important players of "man's most exciting capitalistic game" and that the modern housewife now "reads, for instance, that Wright Aero is going up . . . just as she does that fresh fish is now on the market . . ." The author hazarded the guess that success in speculation would do a lot for women's prestige.) To the typical female plunger the association of Steel was not with a corporation, and certainly not with mines, ships, railroads, blast furnaces, and open hearths. Rather it was with symbols on a tape and lines on a chart and a price that went up. She spoke of Steel with the familiarity of an old friend, when in fact she knew nothing of it whatever. Nor would anyone tell her that she did not know that she did not know. We are a polite and cautious people, and we avoid unpleasantness. Moreover, such advice, so far from accomplishing any result, would only have inspired a feeling of contempt for anyone who lacked the courage and the initiative and the sophistication to see how easily one could become rich. The lady operator had discovered she could be rich. Surely her right to be rich was as good as anyone's.

One of the uses of women is that their motivations, though often similar, are less elaborately disguised than those of men.

The values of a society totally preoccupied with making money are not altogether reassuring. During the summer, the *Times* accepted the copy of a dealer in the securities of the National Waterworks Corporation, a company which had been organized to buy into city water companies. The advertisement carried the following acquisitive thought: "Picture this scene today, if by some cataclysm only one small well should remain for the great city of New York — $1.00 a bucket, $100, $1,000, $1,000,000. The man who owned the well would own the wealth of the city." All cataclysmically minded investors were urged to get a long position in water before it was too late.

v

The polar role of the stock market in American life in the summer of 1929 is beyond doubt. And many people of many different kinds and condition were in the stock market. Frederick Lewis Allen pictured the diversity of this participation in a fine passage:

> The rich man's chauffeur drove with his ears laid back to catch the news of an impending move in Bethlehem Steel; he held fifty shares himself on a twenty-point margin. The window-cleaner at the broker's office paused to watch the ticker, for he was thinking of converting his laboriously accumulated savings into a few shares of Simmons. Edwin Lefèvre (an articulate reporter on the market at this time who could claim considerable personal experience) told of a broker's valet who made nearly a quarter of a million in the market, of a trained nurse who cleaned up thirty thousand following the tips given her by grateful patients; and of a Wyoming cattleman, thirty miles from the nearest railroad, who bought or sold a thousand shares a day.[12]

Yet there is probably more danger of overestimating rather than underestimating the popular interest in the market. The cliché that by 1929 everyone "was in the market" is far from the literal truth. Then, as now, to the great majority of workers, farmers, white-collar workers, indeed to the great majority of all Americans, the stock market was a remote and vaguely ominous thing. Then, as now, not many knew how one went about buying a security; the purchase of stocks on margin was in every respect as remote from life as the casino at Monte Carlo.

In later years, a Senate committee investigating the securities markets undertook to ascertain the number of people

[12] *Only Yesterday*, p. 315.

who were involved in securities speculation in 1929. The
member firms of twenty-nine exchanges in that year reported themselves as having accounts with a total of 1,548,-
707 customers. (Of these, 1,371,920 were customers of member firms of the New York Stock Exchange.) Thus only one
and a half million people, out of a population of approximately 120 million and of between 29 and 30 million families,
had an active association of any sort with the stock market.
And not all of these were speculators. Brokerage firms estimated for the Senate committee that only about 600,000 of
the accounts just mentioned were for margin trading, as
compared with roughly 950,000 in which trading was for
cash.

The figure of 600,000 for margin traders involves some du-
plication — a few large operators had accounts with more
than one broker. There were also some traders whose operations were insignificant. However, some speculators are included among the 950,000 cash customers. Some were putting up the full purchase price for their securities, although
speculating nonetheless. Some were borrowing money outside the market and posting the securities as collateral.
Though listed as cash customers, they were in effect buying
on margin. However, it is safe to say that at the peak in 1929
the number of active speculators was less — and probably
was much less — than a million. Between the end of 1928
and the end of July of 1929, a period when the popular folk-
lore has Americans rushing like lemmings to participate in
the market, the number of margin accounts on all of the exchanges of the country increased by only slightly more than
fifty thousand.[18] The striking thing about the stock market
speculation of 1929 was not the massiveness of the participation. Rather it was the way it became central to the culture.

[18] *Stock Exchange Practices,* Report, 1934, pp. 9, 10.

VI

By the end of the summer of 1929, brokers' bulletins and letters no longer contented themselves with saying what stocks
would rise that day and by how much. They went on to
say that at 2 P.M. Radio or General Motors would be "taken
in hand." [14] The conviction that the market had become the
personal instrument of mysterious but omnipotent men was
never stronger. And, indeed, this was a period of exceedingly active pool and syndicate operations — in short, of
manipulation. During 1929 more than a hundred issues on
the New York Stock Exchange were subject to manipulative
operations, in which members of the Exchange or their partners had participated. The nature of these operations varied
somewhat but, in a typical operation, a number of traders
pooled their resources to boom a particular stock. They ap-
pointed a pool manager, promised not to double-cross each
other by private operations, and the pool manager then took
a position in the stock which might also include shares contributed by the participants. This buying would increase
prices and attract the interest of people watching the tape
across the country. The interest of the latter would then be
further stimulated by active selling and buying, all of which
gave the impression that something big was afloat. Tipsheets
and market commentators would tell of exciting developments in the offing. If all went well, the public would come
in to buy, and prices would rise on their own. The pool manager would then sell out, pay himself a percentage of the
profits, and divide the rest with his investors.[15]

While it lasted, there was never a more agreeable way of
making money. The public at large sensed the attractiveness

[14] Noyes, *op. cit.*, p. 328.
[15] *Stock Exchange Practices*, Report, 1934, p. 30 ff.

of these operations, and as the summer passed it came to be supposed that Wall Street was concerned with little else. This was an exaggeration, but it did not discourage public activity in the market. People did not believe they were being shorn. Nor were they. Both they and the pool operators were making money with the difference, only, that the latter were making more. In any case, the public reaction to inside operations was to hope that it might get some inside information on these operations and so get a cut in the profits that the great men like Cutten, Livermore, Raskob, and the rest were making.

As the market came to be considered less and less a long-run register of corporate prospects and more and more a product of manipulative artifice, the speculator was required to give it his closest, and preferably his undivided attention. Signs of incipient pool activity had to be detected at the earliest possible moment, which meant that one needed to have his eyes on the tape. However, even the person who was relying on hunches, incantations, or simple faith, as distinct from the effort to assess the intentions of the professionals, found it hard to be out of touch. Only in the case of the rarest individuals can speculation be a part-time activity. Money for most people is far too important. Of the South Sea Bubble it was observed that "Statesmen forgot their Politics, Lawyers the Bar, Merchants their Traffic, Physicians their Patients, Tradesmen their Shops, Debtors of Quality their Creditors, Divines the Pulpit, and even the Women themselves their Pride and Vanity!" [16] And so it was in 1929. "Brokers' offices were crowded from 10 A.M. to 3 P.M. with seated or standing customers who, instead of attending to their own business, were watching the blackboard. In

[16] Viscount Erleigh, *The South Sea Bubble* (New York: Putnam, 1933), p. 11.

some 'customers rooms' it was difficult to get access to a spot from which the posted quotations could be seen; no one could get a chance to inspect the tape." [17]

It follows that to be out of touch with the market, ever so briefly, was a nerve-wracking experience. Happily, this was not often necessary. Ticker service was now nationwide; a local telephone call would get the latest quotations from almost anywhere. A journey to Europe provided one of the few troublesome exceptions. As *The Literary Digest* pointed out during the course of the summer, "Transoceanic brokerage business has been growing to immense proportions . . . But there has been an interlude of uncertainty and inconvenience for speculators crossing the ocean." [18] In August even this interlude was eliminated. Progressive brokerage houses — a leader was M. J. Meehan, the specialist in Radio and a veteran of many notable manipulations — installed branches on the big ships under special regulations laid down by the Exchange. On August 17, the *Leviathan* and the *Ile de France* left port fully equipped for speculation on the high seas. Business on the *Ile* the opening day was described as brisk. One of the first transactions was by Irving Berlin, who sold 1000 shares of Paramount-Famous-Lasky at 72. (It was a shrewd move. The stock later went more or less to nothing and the company into bankruptcy.)

In Spokane an anonymous poet on the editorial staff of the *Spokesman-Review* celebrated the seagoing boardrooms.

> *We were crowded in the cabin*
> *Watching figures on the Board;*
> *It was midnight on the ocean*
> *And a tempest loudly roared.*

. . . .

[17] Noyes, *op. cit.*, p. 328.
[18] *The Literary Digest*, August 31, 1929.

"We are lost!" the Captain shouted,
As he staggered down the stairs.

"I've got a tip," he faltered,
"Straight by wireless from the aunt
Of a fellow who's related
To a cousin of Durant."

At these awful words we shuddered,
And the stoutest bull grew sick
While the brokers cried, "More margin!"
And the ticker ceased to tick.

But the captain's little daughter
Said, "I do not understand —
Isn't Morgan on the ocean
Just the same as on the land?" [19]

VII

Labor Day brought the summer of 1929 to its conventional end on September 2. There was a severe heat wave, and on the evening of the holiday returning motorists tied up the roads around New York for miles. In the end many were forced to abandon their vehicles and make their way home by train or subway. On September 3 the city continued to swelter in what the Weather Bureau reported was the hottest day of the year.

Away from Wall Street this was a very quiet day in a very tranquil time. Years later Frederick Lewis Allen went to the newspapers for that day and in a charming article told all that he found.[20] There wasn't much. Disarmament was being discussed in that customarily desultory fashion which

[19] Quoted in *The Literary Digest*, August 31, 1929.
[20] "One Day in History," *Harper's Magazine*, November 1937.

doubtless in the end will destroy us. The Graf Zeppelin was nearing the end of its first round-the-world flight. A tri-motored plane of Transcontinental Air Transport had crashed in a thunderstorm in New Mexico, and eight were killed. (The line had only recently inaugurated a forty-eight-hour service to the West Coast — railway sleeper to Columbus, Ohio, plane to Waynoka, Oklahoma, sleeper again to Clovis, New Mexico, and a plane the rest of the way.) Babe Ruth had knocked out forty home runs so far in the season. As a best-seller, *All Quiet on the Western Front* held a command-ing lead over *Dodsworth*. Women's dresses were all em-phasizing a decidedly flat look without anyone's saying so. From Washington it was announced that Harry F. Sinclair, then in the District of Columbia jail for being in contempt of the Senate during the Teapot Dome investigations, would henceforth be more closely confined. Previously he had been going daily by automobile to the office of the jail physician whom he was serving as a "pharmaceutical assistant." Earlier in the year Sinclair's stock market operations were on a huge scale, and they were later the subject of detailed investigation. It was never shown whether the Washington sojourn in-volved any important interruption. It seems most unlikely that it did. Mr. Sinclair was one of the most resourceful and resilent entrepreneurs of his generation.

On September 3 sales on the New York Stock Exchange were 4,438,910 shares; call money was 9 per cent all day; the rate at the banks on prime commercial paper was 6½ per cent; the rediscount rate at the New York Federal Reserve Bank was 6 per cent. The market was strong with what the market reporters called a good undertone.

American Tel and Tel reached 304 that day. U.S. Steel reached 262; General Electric was 396; J. I. Case, 350; New York Central, 256; Radio Corporation of America, adjusted

for earlier split-ups and still not having paid a dividend, was
505. The brokers' loan figures of the Federal Reserve, when
they were released, also showed another huge increase —
$137,000,000 in one week. The New York banks were also
borrowing heavily from the Federal Reserve to carry the
speculative superstructure — their borrowings during the
week increased by $64,000,000. In August the flow of gold
to New York from abroad had continued large. Yet the new
month seemed to be opening well. There were several expressions of confidence.

On September 3, by common consent, the great bull market of the nineteen-twenties came to an end. Economics, as
always, vouchsafes us few dramatic turning points. Its events
are invariably fuzzy or even indeterminate. On some days
that followed — a few only — some averages were actually
higher. However, never again did the market manifest its
old confidence. The later peaks were not peaks but brief in-
terruptions of a downward trend.

On September 4, the tone of the market was still good, and
then on September 5 came a break. The *Times* industrials
dropped 10 points, and many individual stocks much more.
The blue chips held up fairly well, although Steel went from
255 to 246, while Westinghouse lost 7 points and Tel and Tel
6. Volume mounted sharply as people sought to unload, and
5,565,280 shares were traded on the New York Stock Exchange.

The immediate cause of the break was clear — and interesting. Speaking before his Annual National Business Conference on September 5, Roger Babson observed, "Sooner or
later a crash is coming, and it may be terrific." He suggested
that what had happened in Florida would now happen in
Wall Street, and with customary precision stated that the
(Dow-Jones) market averages would probably drop 60–80

points. In a burst of cheer he concluded that "factories will shut down . . . men will be thrown out of work . . . the vicious circle will get in full swing and the result will be a serious business depression." [21]

This was not exactly reassuring. Yet it was a problem why the market suddenly should pay attention to Babson. As many hastened to say, he had made many predictions before, and they had not affected prices much one way or another. Moreover, Babson was not a man who inspired confidence as a prophet in the manner of Irving Fisher or the Harvard Economic Society. As an educator, philosopher, theologian, statistician, forecaster, economist, and friend of the law of gravity, he had sometimes been thought to spread himself too thin. The methods by which he reached his conclusions were a problem. They involved a hocus-pocus of lines and areas on a chart. Intuition, and possibly even mysticism, played a part. Those who employed rational, objective, and scientific methods were naturally uneasy about Babson, although their methods failed to foretell the crash. In these matters, as often in our culture, it is far, far better to be wrong in a respectable way than to be right for the wrong reasons.

Wall Street was not at loss as to what to do about Babson. It promptly and soundly denounced him. *Barron's*, in an editorial on September 9, referred to him with heavy irony as the "sage of Wellesley" and said he should not be taken seriously by anyone acquainted with the "notorious inaccuracy" of his past statements. The stock exchange house of Hornblower and Weeks sternly told its customers: "We would not be stampeded into selling stocks because of a gratuitous forecast of a bad break in the market by a well-known statistician." [22] Irving Fisher also took issue. He noted that

[21] *The Commercial and Financial Chronicle,* September 7, 1929.
[22] Quoted in *The Wall Street Journal,* September 6, 1929.

dividends were rising, that the suspicion of common stocks
was receding, and that investment trusts now offered the
investor "wide and well-managed diversification." His own
conclusion was: "There may be a recession in stock prices,
but not anything in the nature of a crash." [23] Developing a
slightly different theme, a Boston investment trust told the
public that it should be prepared for slight setbacks, but it
should realize that they would soon pass. In large advertisements it pointed out that "When temporary breaks come,
*indentations in the ever ascending curve of American pros-
perity,* individual stocks, even of the most successful companies, go down with the general list . . . " However, it also
stated on its own behalf that "Incorporated Investors lands
on a cushion."

The Babson Break, as it was promptly called, came on a
Thursday. The market rallied on Friday and was firm on
Saturday. People seemed to be over their fear. It looked as
though the ever ascending curve would start up again, as so
often before and Mr. Babson notwithstanding. Then on the
following week — the week of September 9 — prices were
again ragged. On Monday, the *Times,* with the caution born
of much premature pessimism, hinted that the end had come
and added, "It is a well-known characteristic of 'boom times'
that the idea of their being terminated in the old, unpleasant
way is rarely recognized as possible." On Wednesday, in a
fine example of market prose, the *Wall Street Journal* observed that "price movements in the main body of stocks
yesterday continued to display the characteristics of a major
advance temporarily halted for technical readjustment."

The unevenness continued. On some days the market was
strong; on others it was weak. The direction was slightly,
erratically, but, viewed in retrospect, quite definitely down.

[23] Edward Angly, *Oh, Yeah!* (New York: Viking, 1931), p. 37.

New investment trusts were still being formed; more speculators were flocking to the market, and the volume of brokers' loans continued sharply up. The end had come, but it was not yet in sight.

Perhaps this was as well. The last moments of life should be cherished, as Wall Street had been told. On September 11, in keeping with a regular practice, *The Wall Street Journal* printed its thought for the day. It was from Mark Twain.

Don't part with your illusions; when they are gone you may still exist, but you have ceased to live.

CHAPTER V

The Crash

ACCORDING TO the accepted view of events, by the autumn of 1929 the economy was well into a depression. In June the indexes of industrial and of factory production both reached a peak and turned down. By October, the Federal Reserve index of industrial production stood at 117 as compared with 126 four months earlier. Steel production declined from June on; in October freight-car loadings fell. Home-building, a most mercurial industry, had been falling for several years, and it slumped still farther in 1929. Finally, down came the stock market. A penetrating student of the economic behavior of this period has said that the market slump, "reflected, in the main, the change which was already apparent in the industrial situation." [1]

Thus viewed, the stock market is but a mirror which, per-haps as in this instance, somewhat belatedly, provides an image of the underlying or *fundamental* economic situation. Cause and effect run from the economy to the stock market, never the reverse. In 1929 the economy was headed for trouble. Eventually that trouble was violently reflected in Wall Street.

In 1929 there were good, or at least strategic, reasons for this view, and it is easy to understand why it has become high doctrine. In Wall Street, as elsewhere in 1929, few people wanted a bad depression. In Wall Street, as else-

[1] Thomas Wilson, *Fluctuations in Income and Employment,* p. 143.

where, there is deep faith in the power of incantation. When the market fell many Wall Street citizens immediately sensed the real danger, which was that income and employment — prosperity in general — would be adversely affected. This had to be prevented. Preventive incantation required that as many important people as possible repeat as firmly as they could that it wouldn't happen. This they did. They explained how the stock market was merely the froth and that the real substance of economic life rested in production, employment, and spending, all of which would remain unaffected. No one knew for sure that this was so. As an instrument of economic policy, incantation does not permit of minor doubts or scruples.

In the later years of depression it was important to continue emphasizing the unimportance of the stock market. The depression was an exceptionally disagreeable experience. Wall Street has not always been a cherished symbol in our national life. In some of the devout regions of the nation, those who speculate in stocks — the even more opprobrious term gamblers is used — are not counted the greatest moral adornments of our society. Any explanation of the depression which attributed importance to the market collapse would accordingly have been taken very seriously, and it would have meant serious trouble for Wall Street. Wall Street, no doubt, would have survived, but there would have been scars. We should be clear that no deliberate conspiracy existed to minimize the consequences of the Wall Street crash for the economy. Rather, it merely appeared to everyone with an instinct for conservative survival that Wall Street had better be kept out of it. It was vulnerable.

In fact, any satisfactory explanation of the events of the autumn of 1929 and thereafter must accord a dignified role to the speculative boom and ensuing collapse. Until September or October of 1929 the decline in economic activity was very modest. As I shall argue later, until after the market crash one could reasonably assume that this downward movement might soon reverse itself, as a similar movement had reversed itself in 1927 or did subsequently in 1949. There were no reasons for expecting disaster. No one could foresee that production, prices, incomes, and all other indicators would continue to shrink through three long and dismal years. Only after the market crash were there plausible grounds to suppose that things might now for a long while get a lot worse.

From the foregoing it follows that the crash did not come — as some have suggested — because the market suddenly became aware that a serious depression was in the offing. A depression, serious or otherwise, could not be foreseen when the market fell. There is still the possibility that the downturn in the indexes frightened the speculators, led them to unload their stocks, and so punctured a bubble that had in any case to be punctured one day. This is more plausible. Some people who were watching the indexes may have been persuaded by this intelligence to sell, and others may then have been encouraged to follow. This is not very important, for it is in the nature of a speculative boom that almost anything can collapse it. Any serious shock to confidence can cause sales by those speculators who have always hoped to get out before the final collapse, but after all possible gains from rising prices have been reaped. Their pessimism will infect those simpler souls who had thought the market might go up forever but who now will change their minds and sell. Soon there will be margin calls, and still others will be forced to sell. So the bubble breaks.

Along with the downturn of the indexes Wall Street has

always attributed importance to two other events in the pricking of the bubble. In England on September 20, 1929, the enterprises of Clarence Hatry suddenly collapsed. Hatry was one of those curiously un-English figures with whom the English periodically find themselves unable to cope. Although his earlier financial history had been anything but reassuring, Hatry in the twenties had built up an industrial and financial empire of truly impressive proportions. The nucleus, all the more remarkably, was a line of coin-in-the-slot vending and automatic photograph machines. From these unprepossessing enterprises he had marched on into investment trusts and high finance. His expansion owed much to the issuance of unauthorized stock, the increase of assets by the forging of stock certificates, and other equally informal financing. In the lore of 1929, the unmasking of Hatry in London is supposed to have struck a sharp blow to confidence in New York.[2]

Ranking with Hatry in this lore was the refusal on October 11 of the Massachusetts Department of Public Utilities to allow Boston Edison to split its stock four to one. As the company argued, such split-ups were much in fashion. To avoid going along was to risk being considered back in the corporate gaslight era. The refusal was unprecedented. Moreover, the Department added insult to injury by announcing an investigation of the company's rates and by suggesting that the present value of the stock, "due to the action of speculators," had reached a level where "no one, in our judgment . . . on the basis of its earnings, would find it to his advantage to buy it."

These were uncouth words. They could have been important as, conceivably, could have been the exposure of Clarence Hatry. But it could also be that the inherently unstable

[2] Hatry pleaded guilty and early in 1930 was given a long jail sentence.

equilibrium was shattered simply by a spontaneous decision to get out. On September 22, the financial pages of the New York papers carried an advertisement of an investment service with the arresting headline, OVERSTAYING A BULL MARKET. Its message read as follows: "Most investors make money in a bull market, only to lose all profits made — and sometimes more — in the readjustment that inevitably follows." Instead of the downturn in the Federal Reserve industrial index, the exposure of Hatry, or the unnatural obstinacy of the Massachusetts Department of Public Utilities, it could have been such thoughts stirring first in dozens and then in hundreds, and finally in thousands of breasts which finally brought an end to the boom. What first stirred these doubts we do not know, but neither is it very important that we know.

                                    II

Confidence did not disintegrate at once. As noted, through September and into October, although the trend of the market was generally down, good days came with the bad. Volume was high. On the New York Stock Exchange sales were nearly always above four million, and frequently above five. In September new issues appeared in even greater volume than in August, and they regularly commanded a premium over the offering price. On September 20 the *Times* noted that the stock of the recently launched Lehman Corporation which had been offered at $104 had sold the day before at $136. (In the case of this well-managed investment trust the public enthusiasm was not entirely misguided.) During September brokers' loans increased by nearly $670 million, by far the largest increase of any month to date. This showed that speculative zeal had not diminished.

Other signs indicated that the gods of the New Era were

still in their temples. In its October 12 issue, the *Saturday Evening Post* had a lead story by Isaac F. Marcosson on Ivar Kreuger. This was a scoop, for Kreuger had previously been inaccessible to journalists. "Kreuger," Marcosson observed, "like Hoover, is an engineer. He has consistently applied engineer precision to the welding of his far-flung industry." And this was not the only resemblance. "Like Hoover," the author added, "Kreuger rules through pure reason."

In the interview Kreuger was remarkably candid on one point. He told Mr. Marcosson: "Whatever success I have had may perhaps be attributable to three things: One is silence, the second is more silence, while the third is still more silence." This was so. Two and a half years later Kreuger committed suicide in his Paris apartment, and shortly thereafter it was discovered that his aversion to divulging information, especially if accurate, had kept even his most intimate acquaintances in ignorance of the greatest fraud in history. His American underwriters, the eminently respectable firm of Lee, Higginson and Company of Boston, had heard nothing and knew nothing. One of the members of the firm, Donald Durant, was a member of the board of directors of the Kreuger enterprises. He had never attended a directors' meeting, and it is certain that he would have been no wiser had he done so.

During the last weeks of October, *Time* Magazine, young and not yet omniscient, also featured Kreuger on its cover — "a great admirer of Cecil Rhodes." Then a week later, as though to emphasize its faith in the New Era, it went on to Samuel Insull. (A fortnight after that, its youthful illusions shattered, the weekly newsmagazine gave the place of historic honor to Warden Lawes of Sing Sing.) In these same Indian summer days, *The Wall Street Journal* took notice of the official announcement that Andrew Mellon would remain in the cabinet at least until 1933 (there had been rumors that he might resign) and observed: "Optimism again prevails . . . the announcement . . . did more to restore confidence than anything else." In Germany Charles E. Mitchell announced that the "industrial condition of the United States is absolutely sound," that too much attention was being paid to brokers' loans, and that "nothing can arrest the upward movement." On October 15, as he sailed for home, he enlarged on the point: "The markets generally are now in a healthy condition . . . values have a sound basis in the general prosperity of our country." That same evening Professor Irving Fisher made his historic announcement about the permanently high plateau and added, "I expect to see the stock market a good deal higher than it is today within a few months." Indeed, the only disturbing thing, in these October days, was the fairly steady downward drift in the market.

III

On Saturday, October 19, Washington dispatches reported that Secretary of Commerce Lamont was having trouble finding the $100,000 in public funds that would be required to pay the upkeep of the yacht *Corsair* which J. P. Morgan had just given the government. (Morgan's deprivation was not extreme: a new $3,000,000 *Corsair* was being readied at Bath, Maine.) There were other and more compelling indications of an unaccustomed stringency. The papers told of a very weak market the day before — there were heavy declines on late trading, and the *Times* industrial average had dropped about 7 points. Steel had lost 7 points; General Electric, Westinghouse, and Montgomery Ward all lost 6. Meanwhile, that day's market was behaving very badly. In the second heaviest Saturday's trading in history, 3,488,100 shares were changing hands. At the close the *Times* industrials were down 12 points. The blue chips were seriously off, and speculative favorites had gone into a nosedive. J. I. Case, for example, had fallen a full 40 points.

On Sunday the market was front-page news — the *Times* headline read, "Stocks driven down as wave of selling engulfs the market," and the financial editor next day reported for perhaps the tenth time that the end had come. (He had learned, however, to hedge. "For the time at any rate," he said, "Wall Street seemed to see the reality of things.") No immediate explanation of the break was forthcoming. The Federal Reserve had long been quiet. Babson had said nothing new. Hatry and the Massachusetts Department of Public Utilities were from a week to a month in the past. They became explanations only later.

The papers that Sunday carried three comments which were to become familiar in the days that followed. After Saturday's trading, it was noted, quite a few margin calls went out. This meant that the value of stock which the recipients held on margin had declined to the point where it was no longer sufficient collateral for the loan that had paid for it. The speculator was being asked for more cash.

The other two observations were more reassuring. The papers agreed, and this was also the informed view on Wall Street, that the worst was over. And it was predicted that on the following day the market would begin to receive organized support. Weakness, should it appear, would be tolerated no longer.

Never was there a phrase with more magic than "organized support." Almost immediately it was on every tongue and in every news story about the market. Organized support meant that powerful people would organize to keep

prices of stocks at a reasonable level. Opinions differed as
to who would organize this support. Some had in mind the
big operators like Cutten, Durant, and Raskob. They, of all
people, couldn't afford a collapse. Some thought of the bankers — Charles Mitchell had acted once before, and certainly
if things got bad he would act again. Some had in mind the
investment trusts. They held huge portfolios of common
stocks, and obviously they could not afford to have them become cheap. Also, they had cash. So if stocks did become
cheap the investment trusts would be in the market picking
up bargains. This would mean that the bargains wouldn't
last. With so many people wanting to avoid a further fall, a
further fall would clearly be avoided.

In the ensuing weeks the Sabbath pause had a marked
tendency to breed uneasiness and doubts and pessimism and
a decision to get out on Monday. This, it seems certain, was
what happened on Sunday, October 20.

IV

Monday, October 21, was a very poor day. Sales totaled
6,091,870, the third greatest volume in history, and some
tens of thousands who were watching the market throughout
the country made a disturbing discovery. There was no way
of telling what was happening. Previously on big days of the
bull market the ticker had often fallen behind, and one didn't
discover until well after the market closed how much richer
he had become. But the experience with a falling market
had been much more limited. Not since March had the ticker
fallen seriously behind on declining values. Many now
learned for the first time that they could be ruined, totally
and forever, and not even know it. And if they were not
ruined there was a strong tendency to imagine it. From the
opening on the 21st the ticker lagged, and by noon it was an

hour late. Not until an hour and forty minutes after the close of the market did it record the last transaction. Every ten minutes prices of selected stocks were printed on the bond ticker, but the wide divergence between these and the prices on the tape only added to the uneasiness — and to the growing conviction that it might be best to sell.

Things though bad were still not hopeless. Toward the end of Monday's trading the market rallied and final prices were above the lows for the day. The net losses were considerably less than on Saturday. Tuesday brought a somewhat shaky gain. As so often before, the market seemed to be showing its ability to come back. People got ready to record the experience as merely another setback of which there had been so many previously.

In doing so they were helped by the two men who now were recognized as Wall Street's official prophets. On Monday in New York, Professor Fisher said that the decline had represented only a "shaking out of the lunatic fringe." He went on to explain why he felt that the prices of stocks during the boom had not caught up with their real value and would go higher. Among other things, the market had not yet reflected the beneficent effects of prohibition which had made the American worker "more productive and dependable."

On Tuesday, Charles E. Mitchell dropped anchor in New York with the observation that "the decline had gone too far." (Time and sundry congressional and court proceedings were to show that Mr. Mitchell had strong personal reasons for feeling that way.) He added that conditions were "fundamentally sound," said again that too much attention had been paid to the large volume of brokers' loans, and concluded that the situation was one which would correct itself if left alone. However, another jarring suggestion came from Babson. He recommended selling stocks and buying gold.

By Wednesday, October 23, the effect of this cheer was

somehow dissipated. Instead of further gains there were heavy losses. The opening was quiet enough, but toward midmorning motor accessory stocks were sold heavily, and volume began to increase throughout the list. The last hour was quite phenomenal — 2,600,000 shares changed hands at rapidly declining prices. The *Times* industrial average for the day dropped from 415 to 384, giving up all of its gains since the end of the previous June. Tel and Tel lost 15 points; General Electric, 20; Westinghouse, 25; and J. I. Case, another 46. Again the ticker was far behind, and to add to the uncertainty an ice storm in the Middle West caused widespread disruption of communications. That afternoon and evening thousands of speculators decided to get out while — as they mistakenly supposed — the getting was good. Other thousands were told they had no choice but to get out unless they posted more collateral, for as the day's business came to an end an unprecedented volume of margin calls went out. Speaking in Washington, even Professor Fisher was fractionally less optimistic. He told a meeting of bankers that "security values *in most instances* were not inflated." However, he did not weaken on the unrealized efficiencies of prohibition.

The papers that night went to press with a souvenir of a fast departing era. Formidable advertisements announced subscription rights in a new offering of certificates in Aktiebolaget Kreuger and Toll at $23. There was also one bit of cheer. It was predicted that on the morrow the market would surely begin to receive "organized support."

v

Thursday, October 24, is the first of the days which history — such as it is on the subject — identifies with the panic of

1929. Measured by disorder, fright, and confusion, it deserves to be so regarded. That day 12,894,650 shares changed hands, many of them at prices which shattered the dreams and the hopes of those who had owned them. Of all the mysteries of the stock exchange there is none so impenetrable as why there should be a buyer for everyone who seeks to sell. October 24, 1929, showed that what is mysterious is not inevitable. Often there were no buyers, and only after wide vertical declines could anyone be induced to bid.

The panic did not last all day. It was a phenomenon of the morning hours. The market opening itself was unspectacular, and for a while prices were firm. Volume, however, was very large, and soon prices began to sag. Once again the ticker dropped behind. Prices fell farther and faster, and the ticker lagged more and more. By eleven o'clock the market had degenerated into a wild, mad scramble to sell. In the crowded boardrooms across the country the ticker told of a frightful collapse. But the selected quotations coming in over the bond ticker also showed that current values were far below the ancient history of the tape. The uncertainty led more and more people to try to sell. Others, no longer able to respond to margin calls, were sold out. By eleven-thirty the market had surrendered to blind, relentless fear. This, indeed, was panic.

Outside the Exchange in Broad Street a weird roar could be heard. A crowd gathered. Police Commissioner Grover Whalen became aware that something was happening and dispatched a special police detail to Wall Street to insure the peace. More people came and waited, though apparently no one knew for what. A workman appeared atop one of the high buildings to accomplish some repairs, and the multitude assumed he was a would-be suicide and waited impatiently for him to jump. Crowds also formed around the branch offices of brokerage firms throughout the city and, indeed, throughout the country. Word of what was happening, or what was thought to be happening, was passed out by those who were within sight of the board or the Trans-Lux. An observer thought that people's expressions showed "not so much suffering as a sort of horrified incredulity." [3] Rumor after rumor swept Wall Street and these outlying wakes. Stocks were now selling for nothing. The Chicago and Buffalo Exchanges had closed. A suicide wave was in progress, and eleven well-known speculators had already killed themselves.

At twelve-thirty the officials of the New York Stock Exchange closed the visitors gallery on the wild scenes below. One of the visitors who had just departed was showing his remarkable ability to be on hand with history. He was the former Chancellor of the Exchequer, Mr. Winston Churchill. It was he who in 1925 returned Britain to the gold standard and the overvalued pound. Accordingly, he was responsible for the strain which sent Montagu Norman to plead in New York for easier money, which caused credit to be eased at the fatal time, which, in this academy view, in turn caused the boom. Now Churchill, it could be imagined, was viewing his awful handiwork.

There is no record of anyone's having reproached him. Economics was never his strong point, so (and wisely) it seems most unlikely that he reproached himself.

VI

In New York at least the panic was over by noon. At noon the organized support appeared.

[3] Edwin Lefèvre, "The Little Fellow in Wall Street," *The Saturday Evening Post,* January 4, 1930.

At twelve o'clock reporters learned that a meeting was convening at 23 Wall Street at the offices of J. P. Morgan and Company. The word quickly passed as to who was there — Charles E. Mitchell, the Chairman of the Board of the National City Bank, Albert H. Wiggin, the Chairman of the Chase National Bank, William C. Potter, the President of the Guaranty Trust Company, Seward Prosser, the Chairman of the Bankers Trust Company, and the host, Thomas W. Lamont, the senior partner of Morgan's. According to legend, during the panic of 1907 the elder Morgan had brought to a halt the discussion of whether to save the tottering Trust Company of America by saying that the place to stop the panic was there. It was stopped. Now, twenty-two years later, that drama was being re-enacted. The elder Morgan was dead. His son was in Europe. But equally determined men were moving in. They were the nation's most powerful financiers. They had not yet been pilloried and maligned by New Dealers. The very news that they would act would release people from the fear to which they had surrendered.

It did. A decision was quickly reached to pool resources to support the market.[4] The meeting broke up, and Thomas Lamont met with reporters. His manner was described as serious, but his words were reassuring. In what Frederick Lewis Allen later called one of the most remarkable understatements of all time,[5] he told the newspapermen, "There has been a little distress selling on the Stock Exchange." He

[4] The amounts to be contributed or otherwise committed were never specified. Frederick Lewis Allen (*Only Yesterday*, pp. 329–30) says that each of the institutions, along with George F. Baker, Jr., of the First National, who later joined the pool, put up $40 million. This total — $240 million — seems much too large to be plausible. The *New York Times* subsequently suggested (March 9, 1938) that the total was some $20 to $30 millions.

[5] *Op. cit.*, p. 330.

added that this was "due to a technical condition of the market" rather than any fundamental cause, and told the newsmen that things were "susceptible to betterment." The bankers, he let it be known, had decided to better things.

Word had already reached the floor of the Exchange that the bankers were meeting, and the news ticker had spread the magic word afield. Prices firmed at once and started to rise. Then at one-thirty Richard Whitney appeared on the floor and went to the post where steel was traded. Whitney was perhaps the best-known figure on the floor. He was one of the group of men of good background and appropriate education who, in that time, were expected to manage the affairs of the Exchange. Currently he was vice-president of the Exchange, but in the absence of E. H. H. Simmons in Hawaii he was serving as acting president. What was much more important at the moment, he was known as floor trader for Morgan's and, indeed, his older brother was a Morgan partner.

As he made his way through the teeming crowd, Whitney appeared debonair and self-confident — some later described his manner as jaunty. (His own firm dealt largely in bonds, so it is improbable that he had been much involved in the turmoil of the morning.) At the Steel post he bid 205 for 10,000 shares. This was the price of the last sale, and the current bids were several points lower. In an operation that was totally devoid of normal commercial reticence, he got 200 shares and then left the rest of the order with the specialist. He continued on his way, placing similar orders for fifteen or twenty other stocks.

This was it. The bankers, obviously, had moved in. The effect was electric. Fear vanished and gave way to concern lest the new advance be missed. Prices boomed upward.

The bankers had, indeed, brought off a notable coup.

Prices as they fell that morning kept crossing a large volume of stop-loss orders — orders calling for sales whenever a specified price was reached. Brokers had placed many of these orders for their own protection on the securities of customers who had not responded to calls for additional margin. Each of these stop-loss orders tripped more securities into the market and drove prices down farther. Each spasm of liquidation thus insured that another would follow. It was this literal chain reaction which the bankers checked, and they checked it decisively.

In the closing hour, selling orders continuing to come in from across the country turned the market soft once more. Still, in its own way, the recovery on Black Thursday was as remarkable as the selling that made it so black. The *Times* industrials were off only 12 points, or a little more than a third of the loss of the previous day. Steel, the stock that Whitney had singled out to start the recovery, had opened that morning at 205½, a point or two above the previous close. At the lowest it was down to 193½ for a 12-point loss.[6] Then it recovered to close at 206 for a surprising net gain of 2 points for this day. Montgomery Ward, which had opened at 83 and gone to 50, came back to 74. General Electric was at one point 32 points below its opening price and then came back 25 points. On the Curb, Goldman Sachs Trading Corporation opened at 81, dropped to 65, and then came back to 80. J. I. Case, maintaining a reputation for eccentric behavior that had brought much risk capital into the threshing machine business, made a net gain of 7 points for the day. Many had good reason to be grateful to the financial leaders of Wall Street.

[6] Quotations have normally been rounded to the nearest whole number in this history. The steel quotation on this day seems to call for an exception.

Not everyone could be grateful to be sure. Across the country people were only dimly aware of the improvement. By
early afternoon, when the market started up, the ticker was
hours behind. Although the spot quotations on the bond
ticker showed the improvement, the ticker itself continued
to grind out the most dismal of news. And the news on the
ticker was what counted. To many, many watchers it meant
that they had been sold out and that their dream — in fact,
their brief reality — of opulence had gone glimmering, together with home, car, furs, jewelry, and reputation. That
the market, after breaking them, had recovered was the most
chilling of comfort.

It was eight and a half minutes past seven that night before the ticker finished recording the day's misfortunes. In
the boardrooms speculators who had been sold out since
morning sat silently watching the tape. The habit of months
or years, however idle it had now become, could not be
abandoned at once. Then, as the final trades were registered,
sorrowfully or grimly, according to their nature, they made
their way out into the gathering night.

In Wall Street itself lights blazed from every office as
clerks struggled to come abreast of the day's business. Mes-
sengers and boardroom boys, caught up in the excitement
and untroubled by losses, went skylarking through the streets
until the police arrived to quell them. Representatives of
thirty-five of the largest wire houses assembled at the offices
of Hornblower and Weeks and told the press on departing
that the market was "fundamentally sound" and "technically
in better condition than it has been in months." It was the
unanimous view of those present that the worst had passed.
The host firm dispatched a market letter which stated that

"commencing with today's trading the market should start laying the foundation for the constructive advance which we believe will characterize 1930." Charles E. Mitchell announced that the trouble was "purely technical" and that "fundamentals remained unimpaired." Senator Carter Glass said the trouble was due largely to Charles E. Mitchell. Senator Wilson of Indiana attributed the crash to Democratic resistance to a higher tariff.

VIII

On Friday and Saturday trading continued heavy — just under six million on Friday and over two million at the short session on Saturday. Prices, on the whole, were steady — the averages were a trifle up on Friday but slid off on Saturday. It was thought that the bankers were able to dispose of most of the securities they had acquired while shoring up the market on Thursday. Not only were things better, but everyone was clear as to who had made them so. The bankers had shown both their courage and their power, and the people applauded warmly and generously. The financial community, the *Times* said, now felt "secure in the knowledge that the most powerful banks in the country stood ready to prevent a recurrence [of panic]." As a result it had "relaxed its anxiety."

Perhaps never before or since have so many people taken the measure of economic prospects and found them so favorable as in the two days following the Thursday disaster. The optimism even included a note of self-congratulation. Colonel Ayres in Cleveland thought that no other country could have come through such a bad crash so well. Others pointed out that the prospects for business were good and that the stock market debacle would not make them any less favorable. No one knew, but it cannot be stressed too frequently, that for effective incantation knowledge is neither necessary nor assumed.

Eugene M. Stevens, the President of the Continental Illinois Bank, said, "There is nothing in the business situation to justify any nervousness." Walter Teagle said there had been no "fundamental change" in the oil business to justify concern; Charles M. Schwab said that the steel business had been making "fundamental progress" toward stability and added that this "fundamentally sound condition" was responsible for the prosperity of the industry; Samuel Vauclain, Chairman of the Baldwin Locomotive Works, declared that "fundamentals are sound"; President Hoover said that "the fundamental business of the country, that is production and distribution of commodities, is on a sound and prosperous basis." President Hoover was asked to say something more specific about the market — for example, that stocks were now cheap — but he refused.[7]

Many others joined in. Howard C. Hopson, the head of Associated Gas and Electric, omitted the standard reference to fundamentals and thought it was "undoubtedly beneficial to the business interests of the country to have the gambling type of speculator eliminated." (Mr. Hopson, himself a speculator, although more of the sure-thing type, was also eliminated in due course.) A Boston investment trust took space in *The Wall Street Journal* to say, "S-T-E-A-D-Y Everybody! Calm thinking is in order. Heed the words of America's greatest bankers." A single dissonant note, though great in portent, went unnoticed. Speaking in Poughkeepsie, Gov-

[7] This was stated by Garet Garrett in *The Saturday Evening Post* (December 28, 1929) and it is generally confirmed by Mr. Hoover in his memoirs. According to Mr. Garrett the banker's consortium asked the President for the statement, which suggests that the reassurance, like the support, was tolerably well organized.

ernor Franklin D. Roosevelt criticized the "fever of speculation."

On Sunday there were sermons suggesting that a certain
measure of divine retribution had been visited on the Republic and that it had not been entirely unmerited. People
had lost sight of spiritual values in their single-minded pursuit of riches. Now they had had their lesson.

Almost everyone believed that the heavenly knuckle-rap-
ping was over and that speculation could be now resumed
in earnest. The papers were full of the prospects for next
week's market.

Stocks, it was agreed, were again cheap and accordingly
there would be a heavy rush to buy. Numerous stories from
the brokerage houses, some of them possibly inspired, told
of a fabulous volume of buying orders which was piling up
in anticipation of the opening of the market. In a concerted
advertising campaign in Monday's papers, stock market firms
urged the wisdom of picking up these bargains promptly.
"We believe," said one house, "that the investor who purchases securities at this time with the discrimination that
is always a condition of prudent investing, may do so with
utmost confidence." On Monday the real disaster began.

CHAPTER VI

Things Become More Serious

In the autumn of 1929 the New York Stock Exchange, under roughly its present constitution, was 112 years old. During this lifetime it had seen some difficult days. On September 18, 1873, the firm of Jay Cooke and Company failed, and, as a more or less direct result, so did fifty-seven other stock exchange firms in the next few weeks. On October 23, 1907, call money rates reached 125 per cent in the panic of that year. On September 16, 1920 — the autumn months are the off season in Wall Street — a bomb exploded in front of Morgan's next door, killing thirty people and injuring a hundred more.

A common feature of all these earlier troubles was that having happened they were over. The worst was reasonably recognizable as such. The singular feature of the great crash of 1929 was that the worst continued to worsen. What looked one day like the end proved on the next day to have been only the beginning. Nothing could have been more ingeniously designed to maximize the suffering, and also to insure that as few as possible escaped the common misfortune. The fortunate speculator who had funds to answer the first margin call presently got another and equally urgent one, and if he met that there would still be another. In the end all the money he had was extracted from him and lost. The man with the smart money, who was safely out of the market when the first crash came, naturally went back in to pick up bargains. (Not only were a recorded 12,894,650 shares sold on October 24; precisely the same number were bought.) The bargains then suffered a ruinous fall. Even the man who waited out all of October and all of November, who saw the volume of trading return to normal and saw Wall Street become as placid as a produce market, and who then bought common stocks would see their value drop to a third or a fourth of the purchase price in the next twenty-four months. The Coolidge bull market was a remarkable phenomenon. The ruthlessness of its liquidation was, in its own way, equally remarkable.

II

Monday, October 28, was the first day on which this process of climax and anticlimax *ad infinitum* began to reveal itself. It was another terrible day. Volume was huge, although below the previous Thursday — nine and a quarter million shares as compared with nearly thirteen. But the losses were far more severe. The *Times* industrials were down 49 points for the day. General Electric was off 48; Westinghouse, 34; Tel and Tel, 34. Steel went down 18 points. Indeed, the decline on this one day was greater than that of all the preceding week of panic. Once again a late ticker left everyone in ignorance of what was happening, save that it was bad.

On this day there was no recovery. At one-ten Charles E. Mitchell was observed going into Morgan's, and the news ticker carried the magic word. Steel rallied and went from 194 to 198. But Richard Whitney did not materialize. It seems probable in light of later knowledge that Mitchell was on the way to float a personal loan. The market weakened again, and in the last hour a phenomenal three million shares — a big day's business before and ever since — changed hands at rapidly falling prices.

At four-thirty in the afternoon the bankers assembled once more at Morgan's, and they remained in session until six-thirty. They were described as taking a philosophical attitude, and they told the press that the situation "retained hopeful features," although these were not specified. But the statement they released after the meeting made clear what had been discussed for the two hours. It was no part of the bankers' purpose, the statement said, to maintain any particular level of prices or to protect anyone's profit. Rather the aim was to have an orderly market, one in which offers would be met by bids at some price. The bankers were only concerned that "air holes," as Mr. Lamont had dubbed them, did not appear.

Like many lesser men, Mr. Lamont and his colleagues had suddenly found themselves overcommitted on a falling market. The time had come to go short on promises. Support, organized or otherwise, could not contend with the overwhelming, pathological desire to sell. The meeting had considered how to liquidate the commitment to support the market without adding to the public perturbation.

The formula that was found was a chilling one. On Thursday, Whitney had supported prices and protected profits — or stopped losses. This was what people wanted. To the man who held stock on margin, disaster had only one face and that was falling prices. But now prices were to be allowed to fall. The speculator's only comfort, henceforth, was that his ruin would be accomplished in an orderly and becoming manner.

There were no recriminations at the time. Our political life favors the extremes of speech; the man who is gifted in the arts of abuse is bound to be a notable, if not always a great figure. In business things are different. Here we are surprisingly gentle and forbearing. Even preposterous claims or excuses are normally taken, at least for all public purposes, at their face value. On the evening of the 28th no one any longer could feel "secure in the knowledge that the most powerful banks stood ready to prevent a recurrence" of panic. The market had reasserted itself as an impersonal force beyond the power of any person to control, and, while this is the way markets are supposed to be, it was horrible. But no one assailed the bankers for letting the people down. There was even some talk that on the next day the market might receive organized support.

III

Tuesday, October 29, was the most devastating day in the history of the New York stock market, and it may have been the most devastating day in the history of markets. It combined all of the bad features of all of the bad days before. Volume was immensely greater than on Black Thursday; the drop in prices was almost as great as on Monday. Uncertainty and alarm were as great as on either.

Selling began as soon as the market opened and in huge volume. Great blocks of stock were offered for what they would bring; in the first half hour sales were at a 33,000,000-a-day rate. The air holes, which the bankers were to close, opened wide. Repeatedly and in many issues there was a plethora of selling orders and no buyers at all. The stock of White Sewing Machine Company, which had reached a high of 48 in the months preceding, had closed at 11 the night before. During the day someone — according to Frederick Lewis Allen it was thought to have been a bright messenger boy for the Exchange — had the happy idea of entering a bid for a block of stock at a dollar a share. In the absence of any other bid he got it.[1] Once again, of course, the ticker lagged — at the close it was two and a half hours behind. By then, 16,410,030 sales had been recorded on the New York Stock Exchange — some certainly went unrecorded — or more than three times the number that was once considered a fabulously big day. The *Times* industrial averages were down 43 points, canceling all of the gains of the twelve wonderful months preceding.

The losses would have been worse had there not been a closing rally. Thus Steel, for which Whitney had bid 205 on Thursday, reached 167 during the course of the day, although it rallied to 174 at the close. American Can opened at 130, dropped to 110, and rose to 120. Westinghouse opened at 131 — on September 3 it had closed at 286 — and dropped to 100. Then it rallied to 126. But the worst thing that happened on this terrible day was to the investment trusts. Not only did they go down, but it became apparent that they could go practically to nothing. Goldman Sachs Trading Corporation had closed at 60 the night before. During the day it dropped to 35 and closed at that level, off by not far short of half. Blue Ridge, its offspring once removed, on which the magic of leverage was now working in reverse, did much worse. Early in September it had sold at 24. By October 24 it was down to 12, but it resisted rather well the misfortunes of that day and the day following. On the morning of October 29 it opened at 10 and promptly slipped to 3, giving up more than two thirds of its value. It recovered later but other investment trusts did less well; their stock couldn't be sold at all.

The worst day on Wall Street came eventually to an end.

[1] *Only Yesterday*, p. 333.

Once again the lights blazed all night. Members of the Exchange, their employees, and the employees of the Stock Exchange by now were reaching the breaking point from strain and fatigue. In this condition they faced the task of recording and handling the greatest volume of transactions ever. All of this was without the previous certainty that things might get better. They might go on getting worse. In one house an employee fainted from exhaustion, was revived and put back to work again.

IV

In the first week the slaughter had been of the innocents. During this second week there is some evidence that it was the well-to-do and the wealthy who were being subjected to a leveling process comparable in magnitude and suddenness to that presided over a decade before by Lenin. The size of the blocks of stock which were offered suggested that big speculators were selling or being sold. Another indication came from the boardrooms. A week before they were crowded, now they were nearly empty. Those now in trouble had facilities for suffering in private.

The bankers met twice on the 29th — at noon and again in the evening. There was no suggestion that they were philosophical. This was hardly remarkable because, during the day, an appalling rumor had swept the Exchange. It was that the bankers' pool, so far from stabilizing the market, was actually selling stocks! The prestige of the bankers had in truth been falling even more rapidly than the market. After the evening session, Mr. Lamont met the press with the disenchanting task of denying that they had been liquidating securities — or participating in a bear raid. After

explaining again, somewhat redundantly in view of the
day's events, that it was not the purpose of the bankers
to maintain a particular level of prices, he concluded: "The
group has continued and will continue in a co-operative way
to support the market and has not been a seller of stocks."
In fact, as later intelligence revealed, Albert H. Wiggin of
the Chase was personally short at the time to the tune of
some millions. His co-operative support, which if successful
would have cost him heavily, must have had an interesting
element of ambivalence.

So ended the organized support. The phrase recurred
during the next few days, but no one again saw in it any
ground for hope. Few men ever lost position so rapidly as
did the New York bankers in the five days from October 24
to October 29. The crash on October 24 was the signal for
corporations and out-of-town banks, which had been luxuri-
ating in the 10 per cent and more rate of interest, to recall
their money from Wall Street. Between October 23 and
October 30, as values fell and margin accounts were liquidated, the volume of brokers' loans fell by over a billion.
But the corporations and the out-of-town banks responded
to the horrifying news from New York — although, in fact,
their funds were never seriously endangered — by calling
home over two billions. The New York banks stepped into
the gaping hole that was left by these summer financiers,
and during that first week of crisis they increased their loans
by about a billion. This was a bold step. Had the New
York banks succumbed to the general fright, a money panic
would have been added to the other woes. Stocks would
have been dumped because their owners could not have
borrowed money at any price to carry them. To prevent this
was a considerable achievement for which all who owned
stocks should have been thankful. But the banks received

no credit. People remembered only that they had bravely undertaken to stem the price collapse and had failed.

Despite a flattering supposition to the contrary, people come readily to terms with power. There is little reason to think that the power of the great bankers, while they were assumed to have it, was much resented. But as the ghosts of numerous tyrants, from Julius Caesar to Benito Mussolini will testify, people are very hard on those who, having had power, lose it or are destroyed. Then anger at past arrogance is joined with contempt for present weakness. The victim or his corpse is made to suffer all available indignities.

Such was the fate of the bankers. For the next decade they were fair game for congressional committees, courts, the press, and the comedians. The great pretensions and the great failures of these days were a cause. A banker need not be popular; indeed, a good banker in a healthy capitalist society should probably be much disliked. People do not wish to trust their money to a hail-fellow-well-met but to a misanthrope who can say no. However, a banker must not seem futile, ineffective, or vaguely foolish. In contrast with the stern power of Morgan in 1907, that was precisely how his successors seemed, or were made to seem, in 1929.

The failure of the bankers did not leave the community entirely without constructive leadership. There was Mayor James J. Walker. Appearing before a meeting of motion picture exhibitors on that Tuesday, he appealed to them to "show pictures which will reinstate courage and hope in the hearts of the people."

v

On the Exchange itself, there was a strong feeling that courage and hope might best be restored by just closing up for a while. This feeling had, in fact, been gaining force for several days. Now it derived support from the simple circumstance that everyone was badly in need of sleep. Employees of some Stock Exchange firms had not been home for days. Hotel rooms in downtown New York were at a premium, and restaurants in the financial area had gone on to a fifteen- and twenty-hour day. Nerves were bad, and mistakes were becoming increasingly common. After the close of trading on Tuesday, a broker found a large waste basket of unexecuted orders which he had set aside for early attention and had totally forgotten.[2] One customer, whose margin account was impaired, was sold out twice. A number of firms needed some time to see if they were still solvent. There were, in fact, no important failures by Stock Exchange firms during these days, although one firm had reported itself bankrupt as the result of a clerical error by an employee who was in the last stages of fatigue.[3]

Yet to close the Exchange was a serious matter. It might somehow signify that stocks had lost all their value, with consequences no one could foresee. In any case, securities would immediately become a badly frozen asset. This would be hard on the wholly solvent investors who might need to realize on them or use them as collateral. And sooner or later a new "gutter" market would develop in which individuals would informally dispose of stocks to those increasingly exceptional individuals who still wanted to buy them.

In 1929 the New York Stock Exchange was in principle a sovereignty of its members. Apart from the general statutes relating to the conduct of business and the prevention of

[2] Allen, *op. cit.*, p. 334.
[3] *The Work of the Stock Exchange in the Panic of 1929*, an address by Richard Whitney before the Boston Association of Stock Exchange Firms (Boston: June 10, 1930), pp. 16, 17. Whitney's account, below, of the events of October 29 and thereafter is from the same source.

fraud, it was subject to no important state or federal regulation. This meant a considerable exercise of self-government.
Legislation governing the conduct of trading had to be kept
under review and enforced. Stocks had to be approved for
listing. The building and other facilities of the Exchange had
to be managed. As with the United States Congress, most
of this work was done in committees. (These, in turn, were
dominated by a somewhat smaller group of members who
were expected and accustomed to run things.) A decision to
close the Exchange had to be taken by the Governing Committee, a body of about forty members. The mere knowledge
that this body was meeting would almost certainly have an
unfavorable effect on the market.

Nonetheless, at noon on Tuesday, the 29th, a meeting
was held. The members of the committee left the floor in
twos and threes and went, not to the regular meeting room,
but to the office of the President of the Stock Clearing Corporation directly below the trading floor. Some months later,
Acting President Whitney described the session with considerable graphic talent. "The office they met in was never
designed for large meetings of this sort, with the result that
most of the Governors were compelled to stand, or to sit
on tables. As the meeting proceeded, panic was raging over-
head on the floor. Every few minutes the latest prices were
announced, with quotations moving swiftly and irresistibly
downwards. The feeling of those present was revealed by
their habit of continually lighting cigarettes, taking a puff
or two, putting them out and lighting new ones — a practice
which soon made the narrow room blue with smoke and extremely stuffy."

The result of these nervous deliberations was a decision
to meet again in the evening. By evening the late rally had
occurred, and it was decided to stay open for another day.

The next day a further formula was hit upon. The Exchange would stay open. But it would have some special holidays and then go on short hours, and this would be announced just as soon as the market seemed strong enough to stand it.

Many still wanted to close. Whitney said later, although no doubt with some exaggeration, that in the days to come "the authorities of the Exchange led the life of hunted things, until [eventually] the desirability of holding the market open became apparent to all."

VI

The next day those forces were at work which on occasion bring salvation precisely when salvation seems impossible. Stocks rose wonderfully, miraculously, though still on enormous volume. The *Times* industrials were up 31 points for the day, thus recouping a large part of the terrible losses of the day before. Why this recovery occurred no one will ever know. Organized support can have no credit. Organized reassurance has a somewhat better claim. On the evening of the 29th, Dr. Julius Klein, Assistant Secretary of Commerce, friend of President Hoover, and the senior apostle of the official economic view, took to the radio to remind the country that President Hoover had said that the "fundamental business of the country" was sound. He added firmly, "The main point which I want to emphasize is the fundamental soundness of [the] great mass of economic activities." On Wednesday, Waddill Catchings, of Goldman, Sachs, announced on return from a western trip that general business conditions were "unquestionably fundamentally sound." (The same, by then, could not unquestionably be said of all Goldman, Sachs.) Arthur Brisbane told Hearst readers: "To comfort yourself, if you lost, think of the people living near Mount Pelee, ordered to abandon their homes."

Most important, perhaps, from Pocantico Hills came the first public statement by John D. Rockefeller in several decades. So far as the record shows, it was spontaneous. However, someone in Wall Street — perhaps someone who knew that another appeal to President Hoover to say something specifically encouraging about stocks would be useless — may have realized that a statement from Rockefeller would, if anything, be better. The statement ran: "Believing that fundamental conditions of the country are sound . . . my son and I have for some days been purchasing sound common stocks." The statement was widely applauded, although Eddie Cantor, describing himself as Comedian, Author, Statistician, and Victim, said later, "Sure, who else had any money left?" [4]

The accepted Wall Street explanation of Wednesday's miracle was not the reassurance but the dividend news of the day before. This also, without much question, was somewhat organized. U.S. Steel had declared an extra dividend; American Can had not only declared an extra but had increased its regular dividend. These errant sunbeams were deeply welcome in the dark canyons of lower Manhattan.

Just before the Rockefeller statement arrived, things looked good enough on the Exchange so that Richard Whitney felt safe in announcing that the market would not open until noon the following day (Thursday) and that on Friday and Saturday it would stay shut. The announcement was greeted by cheers. Nerves were clearly past the breaking point. On La Salle Street in Chicago a boy exploded a firecracker. Like wildfire the rumor spread that gangsters whose

[4] *Caught Short! A Saga of Wailing Wall Street* (New York: Simon and Schuster, 1929 A.C. [After Crash]), p. 31.

margin accounts had been closed out were shooting up the street. Several squad cars of police arrived to make them take their losses like honest men. In New York the body of a commission merchant was fished out of the Hudson. The pockets contained $9.40 in change and some margin calls.

VII

At the short session of three hours on Thursday, October 31, well over seven million shares were traded, and the market made another good gain. The *Times* industrials were up 21 points. The weekly return of the Federal Reserve Bank showed a drop in brokers' loans by more than a billion, the largest weekly drop on record. Margin requirements had already been cut to 25 per cent; now the Federal Reserve Banks lowered the rediscount rate from 6 to 5 per cent. The Reserve Banks also launched vigorous open-market purchases of bonds to ease money rates and liberalize the supply of credit. The boom had collapsed; the restraint that had previously been contemplated could now give way to a policy of active encouragement to the market. On all these happy portents the market closed down for Friday, Saturday, and Sunday. They were not days of rest. Brokerage offices were fully staffed, and the Exchange floor was open for completion of trades and also for straightening out innumerable misunderstandings and mistakes. It was noted that on Friday a visitor to the galleries could not have told the market was suspended.

The weekend brought one piece of bad news. That was the announcement on Saturday of the failure of the $20,000,-000 Foshay enterprises of Minneapolis. Foshay owned utilities in some twelve states, Canada, Mexico, and Central America, and an assortment of hotels, flour mills, banks, manufacturing and retail establishments wherever he had happened to buy them. The 32-story obelisk, commemorating the enterprise, which still dominates the Minneapolis skyline, had been opened with fitting ceremony by Secretary of War James W. Good, only in August. (Secretary Good had referred to it as the "Washington Monument of the Northwest.") [5] By all but the most technical of considerations, Foshay was bankrupt at that festive time. His survival depended on his ability to continue merchandising stock to the public. The market crash eliminated this source of revenue and made him dependent on the wholly inadequate earnings of his enterprises.

On all other fronts the news was all good. Alfred P. Sloan, Jr., President of the General Motors Corporation, said: "Business is sound." The Ford Motor Company emphasized a similar conviction by announcing a general reduction in its prices: ". . . we feel that such a step is the best contribution that could be made to assure a continuation of good business." The Roadster was cut from $450 to $435; the Phaeton from $460 to $440; the Tudor Sedan from $525 to $500. For the three days that the market was closed the papers carried stories of the accumulation of buying orders and, in some indefinable way, the stories had a greater ring of conviction than the week before. The market, after all, had closed after an excellent two-day rally. As *Barron's* pointed out, it could now be believed that stocks were selling "ex-hopes and romance." On Monday, the Commercial National Bank and Trust Company took five columns in the *Times* to advertise " . . . our belief and conviction that the general industrial and business condition of the country is fundamentally sound and is essentially unimpaired."

That day the market started on another ghastly slump.

[5] *Investment News*, October 16, 1929, p. 538.

Over the weekend the financial community had almost certainly been persuaded by its own organized and spontaneous efforts at cheer. The papers described the reaction of professional Wall Street to Monday's market as one of stunned surprise, disbelief, and shock. Volume was smaller than the week before, but still well above six million. The whole list was weak; individual issues made big losses; the *Times* industrials were down 22 points for the day. Compared with anything but the week before, this was very bad. When measured against the bright hopes for that day, it was most distressing.

Explanations varied. The rumor recurred that the "organized support" was selling stocks, and Mr. Lamont, on meeting the press, added a minor footnote to this now completed story. He said he didn't know — the organized support was really not that well organized. The most plausible explanation is that everyone was feeling cheerful but the public. As before and later, the weekend had been a time of thought, and out of thought had come pessimism and a decision to sell. So, as on other Mondays, no matter how cheerful the superficial portents, the selling orders poured in in volume.

By now it was also evident that the investment trusts, once considered a buttress of the high plateau and a built-in defense against collapse, were really a profound source of weakness. The leverage, of which people only a fortnight before had spoken so knowledgeably and even affectionately, was now fully in reverse. With remarkable celerity it removed all of the value from the common stock of a trust. As before, the case of a typical trust, a small one, is worth contemplating. Let it be supposed that it had securities in the hands of the public which had a market value of $10,000,000 in early October. Of this, half was in common stock, half in bonds and preferred stock. These securities were fully covered by the current market value of the securities owned. In other words, the trust's portfolio contained securities with a market value also of $10,000,000.

A representative portfolio of securities owned by such a trust would, in the early days of November, have declined in value by perhaps half. (Values of many of these securities by later standards would still be handsome; on November 4, the low for Tel and Tel was still 233, for General Electric it was 234, and for Steel 183.) The new portfolio value, $5,000,000, would be only enough to cover the prior claim on assets of the bonds and preferred stock. The common stock would have nothing behind it. Apart from expectations, which were by no means bright, it was now worthless.

This geometrical ruthlessness was not exceptional. On the contrary, it was everywhere at work on the stock of the leverage trusts. By early November, the stock of most of them had become virtually unsalable. To make matters worse, many of them were traded on the Curb or the out-of-town exchanges where buyers were few and the markets thin.

Never was there a time when more people wanted more money more urgently than in those days. The word that a man had "got caught" by the market was the signal for his creditors to descend on him like locusts. Many who were having trouble meeting their margin calls wanted to sell some stocks so they could hold the rest and thus salvage something from their misfortunes. But such people now found that their investment trust securities could not be sold for any appreciable sum and perhaps not at all. They were forced, as a result, to realize on their good securities. Standard stocks like Steel, General Motors, Tel and Tel were thus dumped on the market in abnormal volume, with the effect on prices that had already been fully revealed. The great investment trust boom had ended in a unique manifestation of Gresham's Law in which the bad stocks were driving out the good.

The stabilizing effects of the huge cash resources of the investment trusts had also proved a mirage. In the early autumn the cash and liquid resources of the investment trusts were large. Many trusts had been attracted by the handsome returns in the call market. (The speculative circle had been closed. People who speculated in the stock of investment trusts were in effect investing in companies which provided the funds to finance their own speculation.) But now, as reverse leverage did its work, investment trust managements were much more concerned over the collapse in the value of their own stock than in the adverse movements in the stock list as a whole. The investment trusts had invested heavily in each other. As a result the fall in Blue Ridge hit Shenandoah, and the resulting collapse in Shenandoah was even more horrible for the Goldman Sachs Trading Corporation.

Under these circumstances, many of the trusts used their available cash in a desperate effort to support their own stock. However, there was a vast difference between buying one's stock now when the public wanted to sell and buying during the previous spring — as Goldman Sachs Trading Corporation had done — when the public wanted to buy and the resulting competition had sent prices higher and higher. Now the cash went out and the stock came in, and prices were either not perceptibly affected or not for long. What six months before had been a brilliant financial maneuver was now a form of fiscal self-immolation. In the last analysis, the purchase by a firm of its own stock is the exact opposite of the sale of stocks. It is by the sale of stock that firms ordinarily grow.

However, none of this was immediately apparent. If one has been a financial genius, faith in one's genius does not dissolve at once. To the battered but unbowed genius, support of the stock of one's own company still seemed a bold, imaginative, and effective course. Indeed, it seemed the only alternative to slow but certain death. So to the extent that their cash resources allowed, the managements of the trusts chose faster, though equally certain death. They bought their own worthless stock. Men have been swindled by other men on many occasions. The autumn of 1929 was, perhaps, the first occasion when men succeeded on a large scale in swindling themselves.

The time has now come to complete the chronicle of the last days of the crisis.

IX

Tuesday, November 5, was election day, and the market was closed all day. In the New York mayoralty race, the Democratic incumbent, James J. Walker, scored a landslide victory over his Republican opponent, F. H. La Guardia, who had been soundly denounced by the Democrats as a socialist. Babson, in a statement, called for poise, discernment, judicious courage, and old-fashioned common sense. On Wednesday the market reopened for the first of a new series of short sessions of three hours. These were the compromise on the question of closing which had been reached the previous week. Nearly six million shares were traded in this session or the equivalent of ten million shares on a full day. There was another sickening slide. U.S. Steel opened at 181, and, by what one paper called a succession of "feverish dips," went to 165. Auburn Automobile lost 66 points; Otis Elevator lost 45. The *Times* industrials were off 37 points for the day, or only 6 points less than on the terrible Tuesday eight days earlier. Where would it all end?

There was also disturbing news from beyond the market. Fundamentals seemed to be turning sour. The week's figures on carloadings showed a heavy drop as compared with the year before. The steel rate was significantly down from the preceding week. More serious, the slump had extended to the commodity markets. On previous days these had reacted sympathetically with the stock market. On this Wednesday they had troubles of their own. Cotton was sharply off in the heaviest trading in weeks. References were made to "panic" in the wheat market when the price dropped vertically at noon.

On Thursday the stock market was steady to higher, but on Friday it took a small drop. People had another weekend of contemplation. This time there was no talk of an accumulation of buying orders; indeed, there was little good news of any kind. On Monday, November 11, came another drastic slump. For the next two days trading was heavy — the Exchange was still on short hours — and prices went down still more. In these three days, November 11, 12, and 13, the *Times* industrials lost another 50 points.

Of all the days of the crash, these without doubt were the dreariest. Organized support had failed. For the moment even organized reassurance had been abandoned. All that could be managed was some sardonic humor. It was noted that the margin calls going out by Western Union that week carried a small sticker: "Remember them at home with a cheery Thanksgiving telegram, the American way for this American day." Clerks in downtown hotels were said to be asking guests whether they wished the room for sleeping or jumping. Two men jumped hand-in-hand from a high window in the Ritz. They had a joint account. *The Wall Street Journal*, becoming biblical, told its readers: "Verily, I say, let the fear of the market be the law of thy life, and abide by the words of the bond salesman." The financial editor of the *Times*, who by this time showed signs of being satisfied with the crash and perhaps even of feeling that it had gone too far, said: "Probably none of the present generation will be able to speak again . . . of a 'healthy reaction.' There are many signs that the phrase is entirely out of date."

CHAPTER VII

Aftermath I

IN THE WEEK or so following Black Thursday, the London penny press told delightedly of the scenes in downtown New York. Speculators were hurling themselves from windows; pedestrians picked their way delicately between the bodies of fallen financiers. The American correspondent for *The Economist* wrote an indignant column for his paper protesting against this picture of imaginary carnage.

In the United States the suicide wave that followed the stock market crash is also a part of the legend of 1929. In fact, there was none. For several years before 1929, the suicide rate had been gradually rising. It continued to increase in that year, with a further and much sharper increase in 1930, 1931, and 1932 — years when there were many things besides the stock market to cause people to conclude that life was no longer worth living. The statistics for New Yorkers, who might be assumed to have had a special propensity for self-destruction, derived from their special propinquity to the market, show only a slight deviation from those for the country as a whole. Since the suicide myth is so well established, it may be useful to give the detailed figures. They are as follows:

NUMBER OF SUICIDES PER 100,000 OF POPULATION
1925–34

Year	For Registration Area *	For New York City
1925	12.1	14.4
1926	12.8	13.7
1927	13.3	15.7
1928	13.0	15.7
1929	14.0	17.0
1930	15.7	18.7
1931	16.8	19.7
1932	17.4	21.3
1933	15.9	18.5
1934	14.9	17.0

* The Registration Area is the part of the country — most of it — wherein causes of death are duly reported. Data are from *Vital Statistics: Special Reports, 1–45, 1935* (Washington: Department of Commerce, Bureau of the Census, 1937).

Since the market crash took place late in the year, there could have been a substantial increase in suicides in late October and thereafter which still would not be great enough to affect the figures for the year as a whole. However, figures on the causes of death by months are also available for 1929.[1] These show that the number of suicides in October and November was comparatively low — in October, 1331 suicides in all the United States, and in November, 1344. In only three other months — January, February, and September — did fewer people destroy themselves. During the summer months, when the market was doing beautifully, the number of suicides was substantially higher.

[1] I am grateful to the custodians of vital statistics in the Department of Health, Education and Welfare for tracking down these figures for me. They are from *Mortality Statistics, 1929* (Washington: Department of Commerce, Bureau of the Census).

One can only guess how the suicide myth became established. Like alcoholics and gamblers, broken speculators are supposed to have a propensity for self-destruction. At a time when broken speculators were plentiful, the newspapers and the public may have simply supplied the corollary. Alternatively, suicides that in other times would have evoked the question, "Why do you suppose he did it?" now had the motive assigned automatically: "The poor fellow was caught in the crash." Finally, it must be noted that, although suicides did not increase sharply either in the months of the crash or in 1929 as a whole, the rate did rise in the later depression years. In memory some of these tragedies may have been moved back a year or two to the time of the stock market crash.

The weight of the evidence suggests that the newspapers and the public merely seized on such suicides as occurred to show that people were reacting appropriately to their misfortune. Enough deaths could be related in one way or another to the market to serve. Beginning soon after Black Thursday, stories of violent self-destruction began to appear in the papers with some regularity. Curiously, though another myth runs strongly to the contrary, few people in these days followed the classical method of jumping from a high window. One would-be suicide jumped into the Schuylkill River, although he changed his mind when he hit the water and was fished out. The head of the Rochester Gas and Electric Company took gas. Another martyr dipped himself in gasoline and touched himself off. He not only made good his escape from his margin calls, but took his wife with him. There was also the suicide of J. J. Riordan.

Riordan's death made large headlines in the newspapers on Sunday, November 10. The papers obviously had sensed a story not only in his death itself, but also in the manner of its announcement. Riordan was a widely-known and popular

figure among New York Democrats. He had been treasurer
of one of Mayor Walker's campaigns and also of one of Al
Smith's. He and Smith were close friends and business associates. Al Smith was a member of the board of directors of
the recently-organized County Trust Company, of which
Riordan was the president.

On Friday, November 8, Riordan went to his bank, took a
pistol from a teller's cage, went home and shot himself. Al
Smith was notified, and his sorrow over the death of his
friend was not diminished by the knowledge that the news
might start a serious run on their bank. A medical examiner
was called but further notification was withheld until the following day (Saturday) at noon, when the bank had closed for
the weekend. There had been a long wake through which
the distinguished mourners had kept one eye on the corpse
and the other on the clock.

The medical examiner first implied that he had postponed
notification out of a feeling of deep responsibility for depositors of the County Trust. This was a formidable exercise of
discretion; carried to its logical conclusion, it meant that all
deaths would have to be weighed by the attending doctor
for their financial consequences. Later it was tacitly conceded that the decision was Al Smith's. So great was Smith's
prestige — and also the general nervousness — that the action was not questioned.

For some days rumors had been circulating that Riordan
had been wiped out by the crash. Now his friends rallied
to his defense, some with vehement assertions that he never
played the market. He had been deeply involved, as subsequent Senate committee investigations of the stock market
revealed, but a hurried audit of the bank showed that all of
its funds were intact. This fact was well-publicized over the
weekend. The City Administration boldly announced that it
was leaving its deposits with the bank, which was a trifle

like saying that it would remain on speaking terms with Tammany Hall. Raskob temporarily assumed the chairmanship. No run developed. The Church concluded that Riordan, a Catholic, had been temporarily deranged and thus was eligible for burial in consecrated ground. Among the honorary pallbearers were Al Smith, Herbert Lehman, and John J. Raskob, and among those attending the funeral were Mayor Frank Hague, Vincent Astor, Grover Whalen, James A. Farley, and M. J. Meehan, the market operator.

Two and a half years later, on Saturday, March 12, 1932, Ivar Kreuger shot himself dead in his Paris apartment at eleven o'clock in the morning local time. This was six hours before the New York Stock Exchange closed. With the cooperation of the Paris police, the news was withheld until the market closed. Later a congressional committee was exceedingly critical of this delay, and Al Smith's action was cited in the defense. In the case of Kreuger, it should be added, the security system of the Paris police was less than perfect. It is fairly certain that there was heavy selling that morning — including heavy short selling — of Kreuger and Toll by continental interests.[2]

II

In many ways the effect of the crash on embezzlement was more significant than on suicide. To the economist embezzlement is the most interesting of crimes. Alone among the

[2] *Stock Exchange Practices,* January 1933, Pt. 4, p. 1214 ff. Such sales were heavy for Friday and Saturday, but in the Exchange records of the time the two days are not segregated. Mr. Donald Durant, the highly uninformed American director of Kreuger and Toll, was in Paris at the time of Kreuger's death and cabled the news to the firm of Lee, Higginson and Company, of which he was a partner. The latter company, which was Kreuger's American investment banker, appears to have refrained scrupulously from acting on the news. *Ibid.,* pp. 1215–16.

various forms of larceny it has a time parameter. Weeks, months, or years may elapse between the commission of the crime and its discovery. (This is a period, incidentally, when the embezzler has his gain and the man who has been embezzled, oddly enough, feels no loss. There is a net increase in psychic wealth.) At any given time there exists an inventory of undiscovered embezzlement in — or more precisely not in — the country's businesses and banks. This inventory — it should perhaps be called the bezzle — amounts at any moment to many millions of dollars. It also varies in size with the business cycle. In good times people are relaxed, trusting, and money is plentiful. But even though money is plentiful, there are always many people who need more. Under these circumstances the rate of embezzlement grows, the rate of discovery falls off, and the bezzle increases rapidly. In depression all this is reversed. Money is watched with a narrow, suspicious eye. The man who handles it is assumed to be dishonest until he proves himself otherwise. Audits are penetrating and meticulous. Commercial morality is enormously improved. The bezzle shrinks.

The stock market boom and the ensuing crash caused a traumatic exaggeration of these normal relationships. To the normal needs for money, for home, family and dissipation, was added, during the boom, the new and overwhelming requirement for funds to play the market or to meet margin calls. Money was exceptionally plentiful. People were also exceptionally trusting. A bank president who was himself trusting Kreuger, Hopson, and Insull was obviously unlikely to suspect his lifelong friend the cashier. In the late twenties the bezzle grew apace.

Just as the boom accelerated the rate of growth, so the crash enormously advanced the rate of discovery. Within a few days, something close to universal trust turned into something akin to universal suspicion. Audits were ordered. Strained or preoccupied behavior was noticed. Most important, the collapse in stock values made irredeemable the position of the employee who had embezzled to play the market. He now confessed.

After the first week or so of the crash, reports of defaulting employees were a daily occurrence. They were far more common than the suicides. On some days comparatively brief accounts occupied a column or more in the *Times*. The amounts were large and small, and they were reported from far and wide.

The most spectacular embezzlement of the period — the counterpart of the Riordan suicide — was the looting of the Union Industrial Bank of Flint, Michigan. The gross take, estimates of which grew alarmingly as the investigation proceeded, was stated in *The Literary Digest* later in the year to be $3,592,000.[3]

In the beginning this embezzlement was a matter of individual initiative. Unknown to each other, a number of the bank's officers began making away with funds. Gradually they became aware of each other's activities, and since they could scarcely expose each other, they co-operated. The enterprise eventually embraced about a dozen people, including virtually all of the principal officers of the bank. Operations were so well organized that even the arrival of bank examiners at the local hotels was made known promptly to members of the syndicate.

Most of the funds which were purloined had been deposited with the bank to be loaned in the New York call market. The money was duly dispatched to New York but promptly recalled while the records continued to show that it was there. The money was then returned once more to New York

[3] December 7, 1929.

and put into stocks. In the spring of 1929 the group was about $100,000 ahead. Then, unfortunately, it went short just as the market soared into the blue yonder of the summer sky. This was so costly that the group was induced to return to a long position, which it did just before the crash. The crash, needless to say, was mortal.

Each week during the autumn more such unfortunates were revealed in their misery. Most of them were small men who had taken a flier in the market and then become more deeply involved. Later they had more impressive companions. It was the crash, and the subsequent ruthless contraction of values which, in the end, exposed the speculation by Kreuger, Hopson, and Insull with the money of other people. Should the American economy ever achieve permanent full employment and prosperity, firms should look well to their auditors. One of the uses of depression is the exposure of what auditors fail to find. Bagehot once observed: "Every great crisis reveals the excessive speculations of many houses which no one before suspected." [4]

III

In mid-November 1929, at long, long last, the market stopped falling — at least, for a while. The low was on Wednesday, November 13. On that day the *Times* industrials closed at 224 down from 452, or by almost exactly one half since September 3. They were also by then down 82 points — about one quarter — from the close on that day barely two weeks before when John D. Rockefeller had announced that he and his son were buying common stocks. On November 13 there was another Rockefeller story: it was said that the family had entered a million-share buying order to peg Standard

4 *Lombard Street,* page 150.

Oil of New Jersey at 50. During the rest of November and December the course of the market was moderately up.

The decline had run its course. However, the end coincided with one last effort at reassurance. No one can say for sure that it did no good. One part was the announcement by the New York Stock Exchange of an investigation of short selling. Inevitably in the preceding weeks there had been rumors of bear raids on the market and of fortunes being made by the shorts. The benign people known as "they," who once had put the market up, were now a malign influence putting it down and making money out of the common disaster. In the early days of the crash it was widely believed that Jesse L. Livermore, a Bostonian with a large and unquestionably exaggerated reputation for bear operations, was heading a syndicate that was driving the market down. So persistent did these rumors become that Livermore, whom few had thought sensitive to public opinion, issued a formal denial that he was involved in any deflationary plot. "What little business I have done in the stock market," he said, "has always been as an individual and will continue to be done on such basis." As early as October 24, *The Wall Street Journal*, then somewhat less reserved in its view of the world than now, complained that "there has been a lot of short selling, a lot of forced selling, and a lot of selling to make the market look bad." Such suspicions the Exchange authorities now sought to dispel. Nothing came of the study.

A more important effort at reassurance was made by President Hoover. Presumably he was still indifferent to the fate of the stock market. But he could not be indifferent to the much publicized fundamentals, which by now were behaving worse each week. Prices of commodities were falling. Freight-car loadings, pig iron and steel production, coal output, and automobile production were also all going down. So, as a result, was the general index of industrial production. Indeed, it was falling much more rapidly than in the sharp postwar depression of 1920–21. There were alarming stories of the drop in consumer buying, especially of more expensive goods. It was said that sales of radio sets in New York had fallen by half since the crash.

Mr. Hoover's first step was out of the later works of John Maynard Keynes. Precisely as Keynes and Keynesians would have advised, he announced a cut in taxes. The rate on both individuals and corporations was cut by one full percentage point. This reduced the income tax of a head of a family with no dependents and an income of $4000 by two-thirds. The man with $5000 got a similar reduction. The tax of a married man with no dependents and an income of $10,000 was cut in half. These were dramatic reductions, but their effect was sadly mitigated by the fact that for most people the taxes being cut were already insignificant. The man with $4000 had his annual tax burden reduced from $5.63 to $1.88. The man with $5000 got a cut from $16.88 to $5.63. For the man with $10,000 the reduction in annual tax was from $120 to $65. The step, nonetheless, was well received as a contribution to increased purchasing power, expanded business investment, and a general revival of confidence.

Mr. Hoover also called a series of meetings on the state of the economy. The leading industrialists, the leading railway executives, the heads of the large utilities, the heads of the important construction companies, the union leaders, and the heads of the farm organizations met in turn with the President during the latter part of November. The procedure in the case of each of the meetings was the same. There was a solemn session with the President, those attending had their picture taken with the President, and there was a press interview at which the conferees gave the press their opinion on the business prospect. The latter, without exception, was highly favorable. After the meeting of the industrial leaders on November 21, which was attended by, among others, Henry Ford, Walter Teagle, Owen D. Young, Alfred P. Sloan, Jr., Pierre du Pont, Walter Gifford, and Andrew Mellon, the expressions of confidence were so robust that Julius Rosenwald, who also attended, said he feared there might soon be a bad labor shortage.

The utility, rail, and construction executives were equally hopeful. Even the heads of the farm organizations were less misanthropic than normal for that time. They said afterward that they had told the President that "the morale of their industry was better than it had been for years."[5]

This was organized reassurance on a really grand scale, and it attracted some of the most enthusiastic comment of the period. A Wall Street financial writer began his story of the sessions: " 'Order up the Moors!' was Marshal Foch's reply at the first battle of the Marne . . . 'Order up the business reserves,' directed President Hoover as pessimistic reports flowed in from all quarters following the stock market crash." The *Philadelphia Record* was led to describe the President as "easily the most commanding figure in the modern science of 'engineering statesmanship.' " The *Boston Globe* said that the nation is now aware "that it has at the White House a man who believes not in the philosophy of drift, but in the dynamics of mastery."[6]

IV

Yet to suppose that President Hoover was engaged only in organizing further reassurance is to do him a serious injustice.

[5] *Magazine of Wall Street*, December 14, 1929, p. 264. The reference to Foch and the Marne following is from the same source.

[6] Both comments are from *The Literary Digest*, November 30, 1929.

He was also conducting one of the oldest, most important —
and, unhappily, one of the least understood — rites in American life. This is the rite of the meeting which is called not
to do business but to do no business. It is a rite which is still
much practiced in our time. It is worth examining for a
moment.

Men meet together for many reasons in the course of business. They need to instruct or persuade each other. They
must agree on a course of action. They find thinking in public more productive or less painful than thinking in private.
But there are at least as many reasons for meetings to trans-
act no business. Meetings are held because men seek com-
panionship or, at a minimum, wish to escape the tedium of
solitary duties. They yearn for the prestige which accrues
to the man who presides over meetings, and this leads them
to convoke assemblages over which they can preside. Finally,
there is the meeting which is called not because there is business to be done, but because it is necessary to create the impression that business is being done. Such meetings are more
than a substitute for action. They are widely regarded as
action.

The fact that no business is transacted at a no-business
meeting is normally not a serious cause of embarrassment to
those attending. Numerous formulas have been devised to
prevent discomfort. Thus scholars, who are great devotees
of the no-business meeting, rely heavily on the exchange-of-
ideas justification. To them the exchange of ideas is an absolute good. Any meeting at which ideas are exchanged is,
therefore, useful. This justification is nearly ironclad. It is
very hard to have a meeting of which it can be said that no
ideas were exchanged.

Salesmen and sales executives, who also are important
practitioners of the no-business gathering, commonly have a

different justification and one that has strong spiritual overtones. Out of the warmth of comradeship, the interplay of personality, the stimulation of alcohol, and the inspiration of oratory comes an impulsive rededication to the daily task. The meeting pays for itself in a fuller and better life and the sale of more goods in future weeks and months.

The no-business meetings of the great business executives depend for their illusion of importance on something quite different. Not the exchange of ideas or the spiritual rewards of comradeship, but a solemn sense of assembled power gives significance to this assemblage. Even though nothing of importance is said or done, men of importance cannot meet without the occasion seeming important. Even the commonplace observation of the head of a large corporation is still the statement of the head of a large corporation. What it lacks in content it gains in power from the assets back of it.

The no-business meeting was an almost perfect instrument for the situation in which President Hoover found himself in the autumn of 1929. The modest tax cut apart, the President was clearly averse to any large-scale government action to counter the developing depression. Nor was it very certain, at the time, what could be done. Yet by 1929 popular faith in laissez faire had been greatly weakened. No responsible political leader could safely proclaim a policy of keeping hands off. The no-business meetings at the White House were a practical expression of laissez faire. No positive action resulted. At the same time they gave a sense of truly impressive action. The conventions governing the no-business session insured that there would be no embarrassment arising from the absence of business. Those who attended accepted as a measure of the importance of the meetings the importance of the people attending. The newspapers also cooperated in emphasizing the importance of the sessions. Had they done otherwise they would, of course, have undermined the value of the sessions as news.

In recent times the no-business meeting at the White House — attended by governors, industrialists, representatives of business, labor, and agriculture — has become an established institution of government. Some device for simulating action, when action is impossible, is indispensable in a sound and functioning democracy. Mr. Hoover in 1929 was a pioneer in this field of public administration.

As the depression deepened, it was said that Mr. Hoover's meetings had been a failure. This, obviously, reflects a very narrow view.

v

In January, February, and March of 1930 the stock market showed a substantial recovery. Then in April the recovery lost momentum, and in June there was another large drop. Thereafter, with few exceptions the market dropped week by week, month by month, and year by year through June of 1932. The position when it finally halted made the worst level during the crash seem memorable by contrast. On November 13, 1929, it may be recalled, the *Times* industrials closed at 224. On July 8, 1932, they were 58. This value was not much more than the net by which they dropped on the single day of October 28, 1929. Standard Oil of New Jersey, which the Rockefellers were believed to have pegged at 50 on November 13, 1929, dropped below 20 in April 1932. On July 8 it was 24. U.S. Steel on July 8 reached a low of 22. On September 3, 1929, it had sold as high as 262. General Motors was a bargain at 8 on July 8, down from 73 on September 3, 1929. Montgomery Ward was 4, down from 138. Tel and Tel was 72, and on September 3, 1929, it had sold at

304. Anaconda sold at 4 on July 8. *The Commercial and Financial Chronicle* observed that "the copper shares are so low that their fluctuations are of little consequence." [7]

However, comparatively speaking, values in these staple stocks had been well maintained. Things were far worse with the investment trusts. Blue Ridge during the week ending July 8, 1932, was 63 cents, and Shenandoah was 50 cents. United Founders and American Founders were both around 50 cents as compared with 70 and 117 (dollars, needless to say) on September 3, 1929. The fears of November 1929 that the investment trusts might go to nothing had been largely realized.

No one any longer suggested that business was sound, fundamentally or otherwise. During the week of July 8, 1932, *Iron Age* announced that steel operations had reached 12 per cent of capacity. This was thought of its sort to be a record. Pig iron output was the lowest since 1896. A total of 720,278 shares were traded that day on the New York Stock Exchange.

Before all this came to pass there had been more, many more, efforts at reassurance. In the weeks of the crash President Hoover had sagely observed: "My own experience . . . has been that words are not of any great importance in times of economic disturbance." This impregnable rule he thereafter forgot. In December he told the Congress that the steps he had taken — the White House no-business conferences in particular — had "re-established confidence." In March 1930, following a flood of optimistic forecasts by his subordinates, Mr. Hoover said that the worst effect of the crash upon unemployment would be ended in sixty days. In May Mr. Hoover said he was convinced "we have now passed the worst and with continued unity of effort shall rapidly

[7] July 9, 1932.

recover." Toward the end of the month he said that business would be normal by fall.[8]

What was perhaps the last word on the policy of reassurance was said by Simeon D. Fess, the Chairman of the Republican National Committee:

> Persons high in Republican circles are beginning to believe that there is some concerted effort on foot to utilize the stock market as a method of discrediting the Administration. Every time an Administration official gives out an optimistic statement about business conditions, the market immediately drops.[9]

[8] Frederick Lewis Allen, *Only Yesterday*, pp. 340–41.
[9] Quoted by Edward Angly, *Oh, Yeah!*, p. 27, from the *New York World* October 15, 1930.

CHAPTER VIII

Aftermath II

THE CRASH blighted the fortunes of many hundreds of thousands of Americans. But among people of prominence worse havoc was worked on reputations. In such circles credit for wisdom, foresight, and, unhappily also, for common honesty underwent a convulsive shrinkage.

On the whole, those who had proclaimed during the crash that business was "fundamentally sound" were not held accountable for their words. The ritualistic nature of their expression was recognized; then as now no one supposed that such spokesmen knew whether business was sound or unsound. One exception was Mr. Hoover. He undoubtedly suffered as the result of his repeated predictions of imminent prosperity. However, Hoover had converted the simple business ritual of reassurance into a major instrument of public policy. It was certain in consequence to be the subject of political comment.

The scholarly forecasters were not so fortunate. People on the whole cherished the discovery that they were not omniscient. Mr. Lawrence disappeared from Princeton. Among economists his voice was not heard again.

The Harvard Economic Society, it will be recalled, had come up to the summer of the crash with a valuable reputation for pessimism. This position it abandoned during the summer when the stock market kept on rising and business seemed strong. On November 2, after the crash, the Society concluded that "the present recession, both for stocks and business, is not the precursor of business depression." On November 10 it made its notable estimate that "a serious depression like that of 1920–21 is outside the range of probability." It repeated this judgment on November 23 and on December 21 gave its forecast for the new year: "A depression seems improbable; [we expect] recovery of business next spring, with further improvement in the fall." On January 18, 1930, the Society said, "There are indications that the severest phase of the recession is over"; on March 1, that "manufacturing activity is now — to judge from past periods of contraction — definitely on the road to recovery", on March 22, "The outlook continues favorable"; on March 29, that "the outlook is favorable"; on April 19, that "by May or June the spring recovery forecast in our letters of last December and November should be clearly apparent"; on May 17, that business "will turn for the better this month or next, recover vigorously in the third quarter and end the year at levels substantially above normal"; on May 24 it was suggested that conditions "continue to justify" the forecasts of May 17; on June 21, that "despite existing irregularities" there would soon be improvement; on June 28 it stated that "irregular and conflicting movements of business should soon give way to sustained recovery"; on July 19 it pointed out that "untoward elements have operated to delay recovery but the evidence nonetheless points to substantial improvement"; and on August 30, 1930, the Society stated that "the present depression has about spent its force." Thereafter the Society became less hopeful. On November 15, 1930, it said: "We are now near the end of the declining phase of the depression." A year later, on October 31, 1931, it said: "Stabilization at [present] depression levels is clearly possible." [1] Even these last forecasts were wildly optimistic. Somewhat later, its reputation for infallibility rather dimmed,

[1] Quotations are from the *Weekly Letters* of the date given.

the Society was dissolved. Harvard economics professors ceased forecasting the future and again donned their accustomed garb of humility.

Professor Irving Fisher tried hard to explain why he had been wrong. Early in November 1929 he suggested that the whole thing had been irrational and hence beyond prediction. In a statement that was not a model of coherence, he said: "It was the psychology of panic. It was mob psychology, and it was not, primarily, that the price level of the market was unsoundly high . . . the fall in the market was very largely due to the psychology by which it went down because it went down." [2] The explanation attracted little attention except from the editor of *The Commercial and Financial Chronicle*. The latter observed with succinct brutality: "The learned professor is wrong as he usually is when he talks about the stock market." The "mob," he added, didn't sell. It got sold out.

Before the year was over, Professor Fisher tried again in a book, *The Stock Market Crash — and After*.[3] He argued, and rightly for the moment, that stocks were still on a plateau, albeit a somewhat lower one than before, that the crash was a great accident, that the market had gone up "principally because of sound, justified expectations of earnings." He also argued that prohibition was still a strong force for higher business productivity and profits, and concluded that for "the immediate future, at least, the outlook is bright." This book attracted little attention. One trouble with being wrong is that it robs the prophet of his audience when he most needs it to explain why.

Out in Ohio, Professor Dice — he of the parasangs — sur-

[2] New York *Herald Tribune*, November 3, 1929. Quoted by *The Commercial and Financial Chronicle*, November 9, 1929.

[3] New York: Macmillan, 1930. The quotations following are on pages 53 and 269.

vived honorably to write and teach for a lifetime about finance.

This may be the place also to record another happy ending. Goldman, Sachs and Company rescued its firm name from its delinquent offspring and returned to an earlier role of strict rectitude and stern conservatism. It became known for its business in the most austere of securities.

II

New York's two greatest banks, the Chase and the National City, suffered severely in the aftermath. They, of course, shared the general obloquy of the New York bankers which resulted from the great hopes and great disappointments of organized support. But it was also the remarkable misfortune of each that it had as its head in those days a market operator in the grand manner.

Of the two, the Chase was the more fortunate. Albert H. Wiggin, variously President, Chairman of the board, and Chairman of the governing board of the Chase, was a speculator and operator, but not an articulate one. However, in 1929 and the years preceding he had been engaging in some astonishing enterprises. In 1929 he received $275,000 compensation as head of the Chase. He was also — or while head of the Chase had been — director of some fifty-nine utility, industrial, insurance, and other corporations and from some of these had also received a handsome salary. Armour and Company had paid him $40,000 to be a member of its finance committee; he got $20,000 a year from the Brooklyn-Manhattan Transit Corporation; at least seven other firms paid him from two to five thousand annually.[4] Wisdom and esteem, or even affection, were not the only

[4] *Stock Exchange Practices,* Report, 1934, p. 201-2.

factors in this compensation. Those who paid were usually clients and prospective borrowers from the Chase. But the most remarkable of Mr. Wiggin's extracurricular interests was a bevy of private companies. Three were personal holding companies, two of which were named sentimentally for his daughters. Three others were incorporated in Canada for highly unsentimental reasons of taxation and corporate reticence.[5]

These companies were the instruments for an astonishing variety of stock market operations. In one operation in the spring of 1929 Shermar Corporation — one of the namesake companies — participated with Harry F. Sinclair and Arthur W. Cutten in a mammoth pool in the common stock of Sinclair Consolidated Oil Company. Even in those tolerant days Sinclair and Cutten were considered rather garish companions for a prominent banker. However, the operation netted Shermar $891,600.37 on no apparent investment.[6]

However, the most breathtaking of Mr. Wiggin's operations were in the stock of the Chase National Bank. These, in turn, were financed by the Chase bank itself. In one exceptionally well-timed coup Shermar Corporation, between September 23 and November 4, 1929, sold short 42,506 shares of Chase stock. (For those to whom short selling is an unrevealed mystery, this meant in effect that it negotiated a loan of 42,506 shares and then sold them at the exceedingly good prices then obtaining. It did this with the intention of buying the same number of shares later at a lower price in order to repay in kind the lender who had provided the original stock. The profit from repaying shares bought at a lower price — always assuming that the price went down

[5] *Stock Exchange Practices*, Hearings, October–November 1933, Pt. 6, pp. 2877 ff.

[6] *Stock Exchange Practices*, Report, 1934, pp. 192–93.

— would obviously accrue to Shermar.) Prices did go down superbly; the short sale anticipated perfectly the crash. Then on December 11, 1929, Murlyn Corporation — this was for another daughter — bought 42,506 shares of stock from an affiliate of the Chase National Bank and financed this purchase with a loan of $6,588,430 from the Chase National Bank and from the Shermar Corporation. These shares were used to cover Shermar's short sale, i.e., to repay the loan of securities. The profits on the operation — at a time when many other people were doing much, much less well — was $4,008,538.[7] People of carping tendencies might hold the profit was earned by the bank, whose stock it was, whose officer Wiggin was, and which had provided the money for the operation. In fact, the gain all went to Wiggin. Mr. Wiggin subsequently defended loans by banks to their own officers to allow them to speculate in their own stock on the grounds that it developed an interest in their institution. However, by this line of reasoning, loans to finance short sales present a difficulty: presumably they develop an interest in having the institution, and hence its stock, behave as badly as possible. Pressed on this point, Mr. Wiggin expressed doubt as to whether officers should sell their own companies short.

At the end of 1932 Mr. Wiggin requested that he not be re-elected Chairman of the Governing Board of the bank. He was approaching sixty-five, and he noted with some slight overstatement that his "heart and energies [had] been concentrated for many years in promoting the growth, welfare, and usefulness of the Chase National Bank."[8] It also seems probable that Winthrop W. Aldrich, who had come into the Chase as the result of a merger with the Equitable

[7] *Stock Exchange Practices*, Report, 1934, pp. 188 ff.
[8] *Stock Exchange Practices*, Hearings, October 1933, Pt. 5, p. 2304.

Trust Company and who represented a more austere tradition in commercial banking — the Equitable was controlled by the Rockefellers — had come to regard Mr. Wiggin as dispensable.[9] The Executive Committee of the Chase, "in order to discharge in some measure the obligations of this bank to Mr. Wiggin,"[10] by unanimous action voted him a life salary of $100,000. It was later brought out that this gesture of inspired generosity had been the impulse of Mr. Wiggin himself. In the months following Mr. Wiggin's retirement his activities became a matter of detailed study by a Senate committee. Mr. Aldrich, his successor, confessed his surprise at the extent and diversity of his predecessor's enterprises and said that the voting of the life salary was a terrible mistake. Mr. Wiggin later renounced the compensation.

III

By comparison with the National City the troubles of the Chase were slight. Mr. Wiggin was a reserved, some described him as a rather scholarly, man. The head of the National City, Charles E. Mitchell, on the other hand, was a genial extrovert with a talent for headlines. He was known to one and all as a leading prophet of the New Era.

In the autumn of 1929 there were rumors in Wall Street that Mitchell would resign. He did not, and the rumors were described by Percy A. Rockefeller, an associate in numerous rather fervent stock market operations and a director of the bank, as "too absurd to be considered by any sensible person."[11] For the next two or three years Mitchell was rather out of the news. Then at nine o'clock on the eve-

---

[9] Mr. Aldrich later told a Senate committee (*ibid.*, p. 4020) that his differences of opinion with friends of Mr. Wiggin, and presumably also with Mr. Wiggin, were a matter of general knowledge.

[10] *Ibid.*, p. 2302.

[11] *Investment News*, November 16, 1929, p. 546.

ning of March 21, 1933, he was arrested by Assistant U.S.
District Attorney Thomas E. Dewey and charged with eva-
sion of income taxes.

Many of the facts were never seriously in dispute. Like
Wiggin, Mitchell had been operating extensively in the stock
of his own bank, although possibly for more defensible reasons. Nineteen-twenty-nine was a year of bank mergers,
and Charles E. Mitchell was no man to resist a trend. By
early autumn of 1929 he had all but completed a merger
with the Corn Exchange Bank. The directors of the two
institutions had approved; all that remained was the for-
mality of ratification by the stockholders. Holders of Corn
Exchange stock were to receive, at their option, four-fifths
of a share of National City stock or $360 in cash. The price
of National City stock was then above 500, so it was certain
that the Corn Exchange stockholders would take the stock.

Then came the crash. The price of National City stock
dropped to around 425, and at any price below 450 —
four-fifths of which equalled the $360 in cash — the stock-
holders of the Corn Exchange would take money. To buy
out all the Corn Exchange stockholders for cash would cost
the National City around $200 million. That was too much,
so Mitchell undertook to save the deal. He began buying
National City stock, and during the week of October 28 he
arranged to borrow twelve million dollars from J. P. Morgan
and Company with which to buy more. (Twelve million was
a sizable sum both for Mitchell and for Morgan's, even at that
time. Only ten million was actually used, and of this four
million was repaid within a week or so. Possibly some of the
Morgan partners had second thoughts on the wisdom of the
loan.)

The coup failed. Like so many others, Mitchell learned
how different it was to support a stock when everyone

wanted to sell as compared with those days but a few weeks back when everyone wanted to buy. The price of National City stock sank lower and lower. Mitchell reached the end of his resources and gave up. This was no time for false pride, and with some mild prodding from the management, the National City stockholders repudiated that management and rejected the now disastrous deal. Mitchell, however, was left with a formidable debt to J. P. Morgan and Company. This debt was secured by the stock that had been purchased to support the market and by Mitchell's personal holdings, but its value was shrinking grievously. By the end of the year National City stock was near 200, down from more than 500, and close to the value at which Morgan's had accepted it as collateral.

Now Mitchell faced another misfortune, or, rather, an earlier piece of good fortune now became a disaster. As an executive of the National City Bank, Mitchell's pay was a modest $25,000. However, the bank had an incentive system which may still hold some sort of record for munificence. After a deduction of 8 per cent, 20 per cent of the profits of the bank and of its security affiliate, the National City Company, were paid into a management fund. This was divided twice a year between the principal officers by an arrangement which must have made for an interesting half hour. Each officer first dropped in a hat an unsigned ballot suggesting the share of the fund that Chairman Mitchell should have. Then each signed a ballot giving his estimate of the worth of each of the other eligible officers, himself excluded. The average of these estimates guided the Executive Committee of the bank in fixing the percentages of the fund each officer was to have.

The years 1928 and 1929 were a time of excellent profits. Mitchell's subordinates had also taken a favorable view of his work. For the full year 1928 his cut was $1,316,634.14. 1929 was even better. The division at the end of the first half of that year brought him no less than $1,108,000.[12] Dividends and numerous other activities had further augmented his income, and all of this meant a serious tax liability. It would have been easy to sell some National City stock and establish a tax loss, but, as noted, the stock was pledged with J. P. Morgan and Company.

Nevertheless, Mitchell sold the stock — to his wife: 18,300 shares were disposed of to this possibly unsuspecting lady at 212, for the exceedingly satisfying loss of $2,872,305.50. This wiped out all tax liability for 1929. Morgan's was not, it appears, notified of the change of ownership of the stock they held. Somewhat later Mitchell reacquired the stock from his wife, also at a price of 212. Before then there had been a further sickening slide in the price, and had Chairman Mitchell bought the stock in the open market rather than from his wife, he could have got it for around 40. Asked about the transaction by Senator Brookhart of Iowa during a Senate hearing, Mitchell, in a burst of candor that must have devastated his lawyer, said: "I sold this stock, frankly, for tax purposes."[13] This frankness led directly to his indictment a few weeks later.

Following his testimony, Mitchell had resigned from the National City Bank. His trial in New York during May and June of 1933 was something of a sensation, although the headlines were necessarily subordinate to the larger ones currently being made in Washington. In his inaugural address on March 4, Roosevelt had promised to drive the money-changers from the temple. Mitchell was widely regarded as the first.

[12] *Stock Exchange Practices*, Report, 1934, p. 206.
[13] *Ibid.*, p. 322.

On June 22, Mitchell was acquitted by the jury on all counts. The sales as required by the tax laws were held to be bona fide transactions made in good faith. The *Times* reporter covering the trial thought that both Mitchell and his lawyer received the verdict with surprise. Attorney General Cummings said that he still believed in the jury system. Mitchell later resumed his career in Wall Street as head of Blyth and Company. The government entered a civil claim for the taxes and won a judgment of $1,100,000 in taxes and penalties. Mitchell appealed the case through to the Supreme Court, lost, and made a final settlement with the government on December 27, 1938. On his behalf it must be stressed that the device by which he sought to reduce his tax liability was far more common then than now. The Senate investigations of 1933 and 1934 showed that tax avoidance had brought individuals of the highest respectability into extraordinary financial intercourse with their wives.[14]

IV

Our political tradition sets great store by the generalized symbol of evil. This is the wrongdoer whose wrongdoing will be taken by the public to be the secret propensity of a whole community or class. We search avidly for such people, not so much because we wish to see them exposed and punished as individuals, but because we cherish the resulting political discomfort of their friends. To uncover an evil man among the friends of one's foes had long been a recognized method of advancing one's political fortunes. However, in recent times the technique has been greatly improved and refined by the added firmness with which the evil of the

14 *Ibid.*, pp. 321, 322.

evildoer is now attributed to friends, acquaintances, and all who share his way of life.

In the nineteen-thirties Wall Street was exceptionally well endowed with enemies. There were some socialists and communists who believed that capitalism should be abolished and obviously did not seek to have its citadel preserved. There were some people who merely thought that Wall Street was bad. There were yet others who did not seek to have Wall Street abolished or who did not care much about its allegedly evil ways but who enjoyed as a matter of course the discomfiture of the rich and the powerful and the proud. There were those who had lost money in Wall Street. Most of all there was the New Deal. The administrations of Coolidge and Hoover had had an extremely overt alliance with the great financial interests which Wall Street symbolized. With the advent of the New Deal the sins of Wall Street became the sins of the political enemy. What was bad for Wall Street was bad for the Republican Party.

For anyone who was in search of symbolic evil in Wall Street — of individuals whose misbehavior would stigmatize the whole community — the discovery that the heads of the National City and Chase had been guilty of grave lapses would seem to be almost ideal. These were the two best-known and most influential banks; what could have been better than default here?

That the shortcomings of Mr. Wiggin and Mr. Mitchell were much welcomed is, of course, clear. Yet in some indefinable sense they were not of that part of Wall Street that people suspected most. Wall Street's crime, in the eyes of its classical enemies, was less its power than its morals. And the center of immorality was not the banks but the stock market. It was on the stock market that men gambled not alone with their own money, but with the wealth of the country. The stock market, with its promise of easy riches, was what led good if not very wise men to perdition — like the cashier of the local bank who was also a vestryman. The senseless gyrations of the stock market affected farm prices and land values and the renewal of notes and mortgages. Though to the sophisticated radical the banks might be the real menace, sound populist attitudes pointed the finger of suspicion at the New York Stock Exchange. There, accordingly, was the place, if possible, to find the symbol of evil, for there was the institution about which people were ready to believe the worst.

The search for a really adequate miscreant in the Stock Exchange began in April of 1932. The task was undertaken by the Senate Committee on Banking and Currency (later by a subcommittee) and its instructions, graced by the usual split infinitive, were "to thoroughly investigate practices of stock exchanges . . ." Under the later guidance of Ferdinand Pecora, this committee became the scourge of commercial, investment, and private bankers. But this was not foreseen when it was organized. The original and more or less exclusive object of the inquiry was the market for securities.

On the whole, this part of the investigation was unproductive. The first witness, when the hearings opened on April 11, 1932, was Richard Whitney.[15] On November 30, 1929, the Governing Committee of the New York Stock Exchange had passed a resolution of appreciation for the "efficient and conscientious" labors of their acting president during the recent storm. It is an "old saying," the Resolution had stated, "that great emergencies produce the men who are competent to deal with them . . ." This sense of indebtedness made it inevitable that when Edward H. H. Simmons retired as President of the Exchange in 1930 after six years in office,

[15] *Stock Exchange Practices,* Hearings, April 1932, Pt. I, p. 1 ff.

Whitney would be elected to succeed him. As President of
the Exchange it thus fell to Whitney, in the spring of 1932,
to assume the task of protecting the stock market from its
critics.

Whitney was not in all respects an ingratiating witness.
One of his successors in office not long ago compared his
general manner and bearing with that of Secretary of Defense Charles E. Wilson at the hearings on his confirmation
as Secretary of Defense in early 1953. Whitney admitted
to no serious fault in the past operations of the Exchange
or even to the possibility of error. He supplied the information that was requested, but he was not unduly helpful to
senators who sought to penetrate the mysteries of short selling, sales against the box, options, pools, and syndicates. He
seemed to feel that these things were beyond the senators'
intelligence. Alternatively he implied that they were things
that every intelligent schoolboy understood and it was painful for him to have to go over the obvious. He was so unwise
as to get into a discussion of personal economic philosophy
with Senator Smith W. Brookhart of Iowa, one of the committee members who believed, devoutly, that the Exchange
was the particular invention of the devil. The government,
not Wall Street, was responsible for the current bad times,
Whitney averred, and the government, he believed, could
make its greatest contribution to recovery by balancing the
budget and thus restoring confidence. To balance the budget
he recommended cutting the pensions and benefits of vet-
erans who had no service-connected disability and also all
government salaries. When asked about cutting his own pay
he said no — it was "very little." Pressed for the amount, he
said that currently it was only about $60,000. His attention
was drawn by the committee members to the fact that this
was six times what a senator received, but Whitney remained

adamantly in favor of cutting the public pay, including that of senators.[16]

In spite of Whitney's manner, or possibly because of it, several days of questioning produced little evidence of wrongdoing and no identification of wrongdoers. Prior to the crash Whitney had heard generally of syndicates and pools, but he could give no details. He repeatedly assured the committee that the Exchange had these and other matters well under control. He took exception to Senator Brookhart's contention that the market was a gambling hell and should be padlocked. In the end Whitney was excused before he had quite completed his testimony.

When the interrogation of Whitney showed clear signs of being unproductive, the committee turned to the famous market operators. These, too, were disappointing. All that could be proved was what everyone knew, namely, that Bernard E. ("Sell 'em Ben") Smith, M. J. Meehan, Arthur W. Cutten, Harry F. Sinclair, Percy A. Rockefeller, and others had been engaged in large-scale efforts to rig the market. Harry F. Sinclair, for example, was shown to have engaged in especially extensive operations in Sinclair Consolidated Oil. This was much like identifying William Z. Foster with the Communist Party. It was impossible to imagine Harry Sinclair not being involved in some intricate maneuver in high finance. Moreover, reprehensible as these activities were, it remained that only three short years before they had been regarded with breathless admiration. The problem here was somewhat similar to that encountered in the great red-hunt of the latter forties. Then there was constant embarrassment over the short time that had elapsed since Red Russia had been our gallant Soviet ally.

[16] *Stock Exchange Practices*, Hearings, February–March 1933, Pt. 6, pp. 2235 ff.

It is true that the big operators, as they appeared on the stand, were not an especially prepossessing group. As noted earlier, Arthur Cutten's memory was extremely defective. M. J. Meehan was in bad health and mistakenly went abroad when he was supposed to go to Washington. (He later apologized handsomely for the error.) Few of the others could remember much about their operations, Napoleonic though they had once seemed. But men cannot be brought to trial for being unprepossessing. And the dubious demeanor and bad memories of the market operators did not directly involve the reputation of the New York Stock Exchange. It is possible to have a poor view of touts, tipsters, and bookies without thinking the worse of Churchill Downs.

In earlier times of trouble on the stock market, stock exchange firms had failed, on occasion by the score. In the fall of 1929 the failures were unimportant. In the first week of the crash no member firm of the New York Stock Exchange had to suspend; only one smallish member firm went under during the period of the panic. There were some complaints by customers of mistreatment. But there were more customers who, during the worst days, were carried by their brokers after their margins had been impaired or depleted. The standards of commercial morality of the members of the Exchange would seem to have been well up to the average of the late twenties. They may have been much more rigorous. This would seem to be the most obvious explanation why the Exchange and its members survived so well the investigations of the thirties. They did not come through unscathed, but they suffered no obloquy comparable, say, with that of the great bankers. In the congressional investigations no flagrant miscreant of any kind was uncovered on the Exchange to serve as the symbolic bad apple. Then, on March 10, 1938, District Attorney Thomas E. Dewey — who had arrested Charles E. Mitchell and who somehow has escaped a reputation as the nemesis of Wall Street — ordered the arraignment of Richard Whitney. The charge was grand larceny.

v

The rush to get in on the act, to use the recent idiom, when Whitney was arrested is a measure of the yearning for a malefactor in the stock market. It can be compared only with the stampede which followed the announcement by Attorney General Herbert Brownell in the autumn of 1953 that former President Truman had shielded treason. On the day following his first arrest, Whitney was arrested again by New York State Attorney General John J. Bennett. Mr. Bennett had been conducting an investigation of Whitney's affairs, and he bitterly accused Mr. Dewey of legal claim-jumping. In the next few weeks virtually every public body or tribunal with a plausible excuse for doing so, called Whitney to enlarge on his wrongdoing.

The detailed story of Richard Whitney's misfortunes do not belong to this chronicle. Many of them occurred after the period with which this history is concerned. There is need here to cover only those operations that were deemed to implicate the market.

Whitney's dishonesty was of a casual, rather juvenile sort. Associates of the day have since explained it as the result of an unfortunate failure to realize that the rules, which were meant for other people, also applied to him. Much more striking than Whitney's dishonesty was the clear fact that he was one of the most disastrous businessmen in modern history. Theft was almost a minor incident pertaining to his business misfortunes.

In the twenties the Wall Street firm of Richard Whitney and Company was an unspectacular bond house with a modest business. Whitney apparently felt that it provided insufficient scope for his imagination, and with the passing years he moved on to other enterprises, including the mining of mineral colloids and the marketing of peat humus in Florida. He had also become interested in the distilling of alcoholic beverages, mainly applejack, in New Jersey. Nothing is so voracious as a losing business, and eventually Whitney had three of them. To keep them going he borrowed from banks, investment bankers, other stock exchange members, and heavily from his brother, George Whitney, a partner of J. P. Morgan and Company. The loans so negotiated, from the early twenties on, totaled in the millions, many of them unsecured. As time passed Whitney was increasingly pressed. When one loan became due he was forced to replace it with another and to borrow still more for the interest on those outstanding. Beginning in 1933 his stock exchange firm was insolvent, although this did not become evident for some five years.[17]

Finally, like so many others, Richard Whitney learned the cost of supporting a stock on a falling market. In 1933, Richard Whitney and Company — the affairs of Whitney and his company were almost completely indistinguishable — had invested in between ten and fifteen thousand shares of Distilled Liquors Corporation, the New Jersey manufacturer of applejack and other intoxicants. The price was $15 a share. In the spring of 1934 the stock reached 45 in over-the-counter trading. In January 1935 it was listed on the New York Curb Exchange. Inevitably Whitney posted the stock as collateral for various of his loans.

[17] These details are from *Securities and Exchange Commission in the Matter of Richard Whitney, Edwin D. Morgan, Etc.*, Vol. I, Report on Investigation (Washington, 1938).

Unhappily, popular enthusiasm for the products of the firm, even in the undiscriminating days following repeal, was remarkably slight. The firm made no money and by June 1936 the price of the stock was down to 11. This drop had a disastrous effect on its value as collateral, and the unhappy Whitney tried to maintain the value by buying more of it. (He later made the claim that he wanted to provide the other investors in the company with a market for their stock,[18] which if true meant that he was engaging in one of the most selfless acts since the death of Sydney Carton.) All the other investors unloaded on Whitney. At the time of his failure, of the 148,750 shares outstanding, Whitney or his firm owned 137,672. By then the value had dropped to between three and four dollars a share. Mention has been made of the tendency of people in this period to swindle themselves. Whitney, in his effort to support the stock of Distilled Liquors Corporation, unquestionably emerged as the Ponzi of financial self-deception. As the result of his operation he had all his old debts, many new ones incurred in supporting the stock, all the stock — and the stock was nearly worthless.

As his position became more complex, Richard Whitney resorted increasingly to an expedient which he had been using for several years — that of posting securities belonging to other people which were in his custody as collateral for his loans. By early 1938 he had reached the end of a surprising capacity to borrow money. Late in the preceding autumn he had had a large last loan from his brother to release securities belonging to the gratuity fund of the Stock Exchange — a fund out of which payments were made on the death of members — which he had appropriated and pledged for a bank loan. He was now desperately, almost pathetically, visiting the most casual of acquaintances in search of funds.

[18] Securities and Exchange Commission, *op. cit.*, Vol. II. p. 50.

The rumor spread that he was in poor condition. Still, on March 8, there was a stunned silence on the floor of the Exchange when President Charles R. Gay announced from the rostrum the suspension of Richard Whitney and Company for insolvency. Members were rather more aghast when they learned that Whitney had been engaged in theft on a large scale for a long period.

With no small dignity Whitney made a full disclosure of his operations, refused to enter any sort of plea in his own defense, and passed permanently from sight.

VI

The failure of the smallest country banker caused more personal hardship, anguish, and privation than the insolvency of Richard Whitney. His victims were almost uniquely able to afford their loss. And the sums which he stole, while substantial, did not place him in the ranks of the great defaulters of the day — they would not have paid the interest on Ivar Kreuger's larceny for a year. Yet, from the point of view of the antagonists of Wall Street, his default was ideal. Rarely has a crime been more joyously received.

Whitney's identification was wholly with the Stock Exchange, the symbolic center of sin. Moreover, he had been its president and its uncompromising defender before the Congress and the public in its period of trial. He was a Republican, an arch-conservative, and was loosely associated in the financial community with J. P. Morgan and Company. He had himself taken a strong position in favor of honesty. Speaking in St. Louis in 1932, at a time when his own larceny was already well advanced, Whitney had said sternly that one of the prime necessities "of a great market is that brokers must be honest and financially responsible." He looked forward to the day when the financial supervision by the Exchange of its members would be so strict that failure "will be next to impossible." [19]

Finally, even by his colleagues, Whitney was regarded as a trifle upstage. In his last days he had been reduced to the ultimate indignity of trying to borrow money from the market operator, Bernard E. Smith. Smith, at best a lower middle-brow figure, later told a Securities and Exchange Commission examiner: "He came up to see me and said he would like to get this over quickly, and told me he would like to borrow $250,000 on his face. I remarked he was putting a pretty high value on his face, so he said . . . his back was to the wall and he had to have $250,000. I told him he had a lot of nerve to ask me for $250,000 when he didn't even bid me the time of day. I told him I frankly didn't like him — that I wouldn't loan him a dime." [20] On any free vote for the man best qualified to bring discredit to Wall Street, Whitney would have won by a wide margin.

The parallel between Whitney and a more recent culprit is interesting. During the thirties the New Dealers were exuberantly uncovering the financial derelictions of their opposition. (It is interesting that dishonesty and not the more orthodox offenses of capitalism like abuse of power or the exploitation of the people were in these days the nemesis of conservatives.) In the nineteen-forties and fifties Republicans, as avidly, were discovering that there were New Dealers who had been communists. Thus it came about that a decade later the counterpart of Richard Whitney was Alger Hiss.

[19] *The New York Stock Exchange,* an address by Richard Whitney before the Industrial Club of St. Louis and the Chamber of Commerce of St. Louis (St. Louis, September 27, 1932).

[20] Securities and Exchange Commission, *op. cit.,* Transcript of Hearings, Vol. II, pp. 822, 823.

Each served admirably the enemies of his class. Each in origin, education, associations, and career pretension epitomized that class. In each case the first reaction of friends to the allegations of guilt was disbelief. Whitney's past role in his community had been more prominent, and hence from the viewpoint of his enemies he was a more satisfactory figure than Alger Hiss. In the government hierarchy, Hiss was a distinctly routine figure. His eminence as a global statesman was synthesized *ex post facto* and he also gained much prominence during two long trials. Whitney, with no fanfare, accepted his fate.

There is, perhaps, a moral worth drawing from the careers of Whitney and Hiss. Neither the fact that Whitney was convicted of purloining securities nor that Hiss purloined documents is convincing proof that their friends, associates, and contemporaries were doing the same. On the contrary, the evidence would indicate that most brokers were honest as a matter of absolute routine, and most New Dealers, so far from being in league with the Russians, wished only that they might be invited once to taste caviar at the Soviet embassy. Both liberals and conservatives, left and right, have now had personal experience with the use of the symbolic evil. The injustice of the device is evident. What may be a more compelling point, so are its dangers. In accordance with an old but not outworn tradition, it might now be wise for all to conclude that crime, or even misbehavior, is the act of an individual, not the predisposition of a class.

VII

The Whitney affair brought a marked change in the relations between the Exchange and the federal government, and, in some measure, between the Exchange and the general public. In the Securities Act of 1933, and more comprehensively in the Securities Exchange Act of 1934, the government had sought to prohibit some of the more spectacular extravagances of 1928 and 1929. Full disclosure was required on new security issues, although no way was found of making would-be investors read what was disclosed. Inside operations and short selling after the manner of Mr. Wiggin were outlawed. Authority was given to the Federal Reserve Board to fix margin requirements and these could, if necessary, be made 100 per cent and thus eliminate margin trading entirely. Pool operations, wash sales, the dissemination of tips or patently false information and other devices for rigging or manipulating the market were prohibited. Commercial banks were divorced from their securities affiliates. Most important, the principle was enunciated that the New York Stock Exchange and the other exchanges were subject to public regulation and the Securities and Exchange Commission was established to apply and enforce such regulation.

This was somewhat bitter medicine. Moreover, regulatory bodies, like the people who comprise them, have a marked life cycle. In youth they are vigorous, aggressive, evangelistic, and even intolerant. Later they mellow, and in old age — after a matter of ten or fifteen years — they become, with some exceptions, either an arm of the industry they are regulating or senile. The SEC was especially aggressive. To any young regulatory body, after all, Wall Street was certain to seem a challenging antagonist.

Until the Whitney affair Wall Street — always with exceptions — was disposed to fight back. It insisted on the right of a financial community in general, and of a securities market in particular, to conduct its affairs in its own way, by its own lights and to govern itself. On the evening before the suspension of Whitney was announced from the rostrum,

Charles R. Gay, the President of the Exchange, and Howland S. Davis, Chairman of the Committee on Business Conduct — Whitney had been a predecessor of both in the two offices — made their way to Washington. There they reported their unhappy news to William O. Douglas and John W. Hanes of the SEC. The trip, in far more than a symbolic sense, represented the surrender of the Exchange. The cold war over regulation came to an end and was not thereafter resumed.

While the Whitney default confirmed the victory of the New Deal on the issue of regulation and also served admirably to confirm the more general suspicion of moral delinquency in downtown New York, it was Wall Street's good fortune that it came late. By 1938 the New Deal assault on big business was on the wane; some leaders of the original shock troops were already polishing up speeches on the virtues of the free enterprise system. By then, also, it was accepted New Deal theology that all necessary economic reforms had been revealed and those that had not been enacted were on request from Congress. No further reforms of the securities markets of any importance were on the agenda. Henceforth Wall Street looked ingratiatingly at Washington and Washington merely looked blank.

CHAPTER IX

Cause and Consequence

AFTER THE Great Crash came the Great Depression which lasted, with varying severity, for ten years. In 1933, Gross National Product (total production of the economy) was nearly a third less than in 1929. Not until 1937 did the physical volume of production recover to the levels of 1929, and then it promptly slipped back again. Until 1941 the dollar value of production remained below 1929. Between 1930 and 1940 only once, in 1937, did the average number unemployed during the year drop below eight million. In 1933 nearly thirteen million were out of work, or about one in every four in the labor force. In 1938 one person in five was still out of work.[1]

It was during this dreary time that 1929 became a year of myth. People hoped that the country might get back to twenty-nine; in some industries or towns when business was phenomenally good it was almost as good as in twenty-nine; men of outstanding vision, on occasions of exceptional solemnity, were heard to say that 1929 "was no better than Americans deserve."

On the whole, the great stock market crash can be much more readily explained than the depression that followed it. And among the problems involved in assessing the causes of depression none is more intractable than the responsibility

[1] *Economic Indicators: Historical and Descriptive Supplement*, Joint Committee on the Economic Report (Washington, 1953).

to be assigned to the stock market crash. Economics still does not allow final answers on these matters. But, as usual, something can be said.

II

As already so often emphasized, the collapse in the stock market in the autumn of 1929 was implicit in the speculation that went before. The only question concerning that speculation was how long it would last. Sometime, sooner or later, confidence in the short-run reality of increasing common stock values would weaken. When this happened, some people would sell, and this would destroy the reality of increasing values. Holding for an increase would now become meaningless; the new reality would be falling prices. There would be a rush, pellmell, to unload. This was the way past speculative orgies had ended. It was the way the end came in 1929. It is the way speculation will end in the future.

We do not know why a great speculative orgy occurred in 1928 and 1929. The long accepted explanation that credit was easy and so people were impelled to borrow money to buy common stocks on margin is obviously nonsense. On numerous occasions before and since credit has been easy, and there has been no speculation whatever. Furthermore, much of the 1928 and 1929 speculation occurred on money borrowed at interest rates which for years before, and in any period since, would have been considered exceptionally astringent. Money, by the ordinary tests, was tight in the late twenties.

Far more important than rate of interest and the supply of credit is the mood. Speculation on a large scale requires a pervasive sense of confidence and optimism and conviction that ordinary people were meant to be rich. People must also have faith in the good intentions and even in the benevolence of others, for it is by the agency of others that they will get rich. In 1929 Professor Dice observed: "The common folks believe in their leaders. We no longer look upon the captains of industry as magnified crooks. Have we not heard their voices over the radio? Are we not familiar with their thoughts, ambitions, and ideals as they have expressed them to us almost as a man talks to his friend?" [2] Such a feeling of trust is essential for a boom. When people are cautious, questioning, misanthropic, suspicious, or mean, they are immune to speculative enthusiasms.

Savings must also be plentiful. Speculation, however it may rely on borrowed funds, must be nourished in part by those who participate. If savings are growing rapidly, people will place a lower marginal value on their accumulation; they will be willing to risk some of it against the prospect of a greatly enhanced return. Speculation, accordingly, is most likely to break out after a substantial period of prosperity, rather than in the early phases of recovery from a depression. Macaulay noted that between the Restoration and the Glorious Revolution Englishmen were at loss to know what to do with their savings and that the "natural effect of this state of things was that a crowd of projectors, ingenious and absurd, honest and knavish, employed themselves in devising new schemes for the employment of redundant capital." Bagehot and others have attributed the South Sea Bubble to roughly the same causes. [3] In 1720 England had enjoyed a long period of prosperity, enhanced in part by war expenditures, and during this time private savings are believed to have grown at an unprecedented rate. Investment outlets

[2] *New Levels in the Stock Market*, p. 257.

[3] Walter Bagehot, *Lombard Street*, p. 130. The quotation from Macauli y, above, is cited by Bagehot, p. 128.

were also few and returns low. Accordingly, Englishmen were anxious to place their savings at the disposal of the new enterprises and were quick to believe that the prospects were not fantastic. So it was in 1928 and 1929.

Finally, a speculative outbreak has a greater or less immunizing effect. The ensuing collapse automatically destroys the very mood speculation requires. It follows that an outbreak of speculation provides a reasonable assurance that another outbreak will not immediately occur. With time and the dimming of memory, the immunity wears off. A recurrence becomes possible. Nothing would have induced Americans to launch a speculative adventure in the stock market in 1935. By 1955 the chances are very much better.

III

As noted, it is easier to account for the boom and crash in the market than to explain their bearing on the depression which followed. The causes of the Great Depression are still far from certain. A lack of certainty, it may also be observed, is not evident in the contemporary writing on the subject. Much of it tells what went wrong and why with marked firmness. However, this paradoxically can itself be an indication of uncertainty. When people are least sure they are often most dogmatic. We do not know what the Russians intend, so we state with great assurance what they will do. We compensate for our inability to foretell the consequences of, say, rearming Germany by asserting positively just what the consequences will be. So it is in economics. Yet, in explaining what happened in 1929 and after, one can distinguish between explanations that might be right and those that are clearly wrong.

A great many people have always felt that a depression was inevitable in the thirties. There had been (at least) seven good years; now by an occult or biblical law of compensation there would have to be seven bad ones. Perhaps, consciously or unconsciously, an argument that was valid for the stock market was brought to bear on the economy in general. Because the market took leave of reality in 1928 and 1929, it had at some time to make a return to reality. The disenchantment was bound to be as painful as the illusions were beguiling. Similarly, the New Era prosperity would some day evaporate; in its wake would come the compensating hardship.

There is also the slightly more subtle conviction that economic life is governed by an inevitable rhythm. After a certain time prosperity destroys itself and depression corrects itself. In 1929 prosperity, in accordance with the dictates of the business cycle, had run its course. This was the faith confessed by the members of the Harvard Economic Society in the spring of 1929 when they concluded that a recession was somehow overdue.

Neither of these beliefs can be seriously supported. The twenties by being comparatively prosperous established no imperative that the thirties be depressed. In the past, good times have given way to less good times and less good or bad to good. But change is normal in a capitalist economy. The degree of regularity in such movements is not great, though often thought to be.[4] No inevitable rhythm required the collapse and stagnation of 1930-40.

Nor was the economy of the United States in 1929 subject

---

[4] "At present it is less likely that the existence of business cycles will be denied than that their regularity will be exaggerated." Wesley Clair Mitchell, *Business Cycles and Unemployment* (New York: McGraw-Hill, 1923), p. 6.

to such physical pressure or strain as the result of its past level of performance that a depression was bound to come. The notion that the economy requires occasional rest and resuscitation has a measure of plausibility and also a marked viability. During the summer of 1954 a professional economist on President Eisenhower's personal staff explained the then current recession by saying that the economy was enjoying a brief (and presumably well-merited) rest after the exceptional exertions of preceding years. In 1929 the labor force was not tired; it could have continued to produce indefinitely at the best 1929 rate. The capital plant of the country was not depleted. In the preceding years of prosperity, plant had been renewed and improved. In fact, depletion of the capital plant occurred during the ensuing years of idleness when new investment was sharply curtailed. Raw materials in 1929 were ample for the current rate of production. Entrepreneurs were never more eupeptic. Obviously if men, materials, plant, and management were all capable of continued and even enlarged exertions a refreshing pause was not necessary.

Finally, the high production of the twenties did not, as some have suggested, outrun the wants of the people. During these years people were indeed being supplied with an increasing volume of goods. But there is no evidence that their desire for automobiles, clothing, travel, recreation, or even food was sated. On the contrary, all subsequent evidence showed (given the income to spend) a capacity for a large further increase in consumption. A depression was not needed so that people's wants could catch up with their capacity to produce.

IV

What, then, are the plausible causes of the depression? The task of answering can be simplified somewhat by dividing the problem into two parts. First there is the question of why economic activity turned down in 1929. Second there is the vastly more important question of why, having started down, on this unhappy occasion it went down and down and down and remained low for a full decade.

As noted, the Federal Reserve indexes of industrial activity and of factory production, the most comprehensive monthly measures of economic activity then available, reached a peak in June. They then turned down and continued to decline throughout the rest of the year. The turning point in other indicators — factory payrolls, freight-car loadings, and department store sales — came later, and it was October or after before the trend in all of them was clearly down. Still, as economists have generally insisted, and the matter has the high authority of the National Bureau of Economic Research,[5] the economy had weakened in the early summer well before the crash.

This weakening can be variously explained. Production of industrial products, for the moment, had outrun consumer and investment demand for them. The most likely reason is that business concerns, in the characteristic enthusiasm of good times, misjudged the prospective increase in demand and acquired larger inventories than they later found they needed. As a result they curtailed their buying, and this led to a cutback in production. In short, the summer of 1929 marked the beginning of the familiar inventory recession. The proof is not conclusive from the (by present standards)

[5] Geoffrey H. Moore, *Statistical Indications of Cyclical Revivals and Recessions, Occasional Paper 31*, National Bureau of Economic Research, Inc. (New York, 1950).

limited figures available. Department store inventories, for which figures are available, seem not to have been out of line early in the year. But a mild slump in department store sales in April could have been a signal for curtailment.

Also there is a chance — one that students of the period have generally favored — that more deep-seated factors were at work and made themselves seriously evident for the first time during that summer. Throughout the twenties production and productivity per worker grew steadily: between 1919 and 1929, output per worker in manufacturing industries increased by about 43 per cent.[6] Wages, salaries, and prices all remained comparatively stable, or in any case underwent no comparable increase. Accordingly, costs fell and with prices the same, profits increased. These profits sustained the spending of the well-to-do, and they also nourished at least some of the expectations behind the stock market boom. Most of all they encouraged a very high level of capital investment. During the twenties, the production of capital goods increased at an average annual rate of 6.4 per cent a year; non-durable consumers' goods, a category which includes such objects of mass consumption as food and clothing, increased at a rate of only 2.8 per cent.[7] (The rate of increase for durable consumers' goods such as cars, dwellings, home furnishings, and the like, much of it representing expenditures of the well-off to well-to-do, was 5.9 per cent.) A large and increasing investment in capital goods was, in other words, a principal device by which the profits were being spent.[8] It follows that anything that in-

[6] H. W. Arndt, *The Economic Lessons of the Nineteen-Thirties* (London: Oxford, 1944), p. 15.

[7] E. M. Hugh-Jones and E. A. Radice, *An American Experiment* (London: Oxford, 1936), 49. Cited by Arndt, *op. cit.*, p. 16.

[8] This has been widely noted. See Lionel Robbins, *The Great Depression*, p. 4, and Thomas Wilson, *Fluctuations in Income*, p. 154 ff., and J. M. Keynes, *A Treatise on Money* (New York: Harcourt, Brace, 1930), II, 190 ff.

terrupted the investment outlays — anything, indeed, which kept them from showing the necessary rate of increase — could cause trouble. When this occurred, compensation through an increase in consumer spending could not automatically be expected. The effect, therefore, of insufficient investment — investment that failed to keep pace with the steady increase in profits — could be falling total demand reflected in turn in falling orders and output. Again there is no final proof of this point, for unfortunately we do not know how rapidly investment had to grow to keep abreast of the current increase in profits.[9] However, the explanation is broadly consistent with the facts.

There are other possible explanations of the downturn. Back of the insufficient advance in investment may have been the high interest rates. Perhaps, although less probably, trouble was transmitted to the economy as a whole from some weak sector like agriculture. Further explanations could be offered. But one thing about this experience is clear. Until well along in the autumn of 1929 the downturn was limited. The recession in business activity was modest and underemployment relatively slight. Up to November it

[9] Perhaps I may be permitted to enlarge on this in slightly more technical terms. The interruption could as well have been caused by an insufficient rate of increase in consumer spending as by a failure in the greater rate of increase of capital goods spending. Under-consumption and under-investment are the same side of the same coin. And some force is added to this explanation by the fact that spending for one important consumers' durable, namely houses, had been declining for several years and suffered a further substantial drop in 1929. However, the investment function we still suppose to be less stable than the consumption function, even though we are less assured of the stability of the latter than we used to be. And in the present case it seems wise to attach causal significance to the part of the spending which had to maintain the largest rate of increase if total spending were to be uninterrupted. The need to maintain a specific rate of increase in investment outlay is insufficiently emphasized by Mr. Thomas Wilson in his book which I have so frequently cited and to which students of the period are indebted.

was possible to argue that not much of anything had happened. On other occasions, as noted — in 1924 and 1927 and of late in 1949 — the economy has undergone similar recession. But, unlike these other occasions, in 1929 the recession continued and continued and got violently worse. This is the unique feature of the 1929 experience. This is what we need really to understand.

v

There seems little question that in 1929, modifying a famous cliché, the economy was fundamentally unsound. This is a circumstance of first-rate importance. Many things were wrong, but five weaknesses seem to have had an especially intimate bearing on the ensuing disaster. They are:

1) The bad distribution of income. In 1929 the rich were indubitably rich. The figures are not entirely satisfactory, but it seems certain that the 5 per cent of the population with the highest incomes in that year received approximately one third of all personal income. The proportion of personal income received in the form of interest, dividends, and rent — the income, broadly speaking, of the well-to-do — was about twice as great as in the years following the Second World War.[10]

This highly unequal income distribution meant that the economy was dependent on a high level of investment or a high level of luxury consumer spending or both. The rich cannot buy great quantities of bread. If they are to dispose of what they receive it must be on luxuries or by way of investment in new plants and new projects. Both investment and luxury spending are subject, inevitably, to more

[10] Selma Goldsmith, George Jaszi, Hyman Kaitz, and Maurice Liebenberg, "Size Distribution of Income since the Mid-Thirties," *The Review of Economics and Statistics*, February 1954, pp. 16, 18

erratic influences and to wider fluctuations than the bread
and rent outlays of the $25-a-week workman. This high-
bracket spending and investment was especially susceptible,
one may assume, to the crushing news from the stock market
in October of 1929.

2) The bad corporate structure. In November 1929, a few
weeks after the crash, the Harvard Economic Society gave as
a principal reason why a depression need not be feared its
reasoned judgment that "business in most lines has been conducted with prudence and conservatism." [11] The fact was that
American enterprise in the twenties had opened its hos-
pitable arms to an exceptional number of promoters, grafters,
swindlers, impostors, and frauds. This, in the long history
of such activities, was a kind of flood tide of corporate larceny.

The most important corporate weakness was inherent in
the vast new structure of holding companies and investment
trusts. The holding companies controlled large segments of
the utility, railroad, and entertainment business. Here, as
with the investment trusts, was the constant danger of devastation by reverse leverage. In particular, dividends from
the operating companies paid the interest on the bonds of
upstream holding companies. The interruption of the dividends meant default on the bonds, bankruptcy, and the collapse of the structure. Under these circumstances, the temp-
tation to curtail investment in operating plant in order to
continue dividends was obviously strong. This added to
deflationary pressures. The latter, in turn, curtailed earnings
and helped bring down the corporate pyramids. When this
happened, even more retrenchment was inevitable. Income
was earmarked for debt repayment. Borrowing for new investment became impossible. It would be hard to imagine a

[11] *Weekly Letter,* November 23, 1929.

corporate system better designed to continue and accentuate a deflationary spiral.

3) The bad banking structure. Since the early thirties, a generation of Americans has been told, sometimes with amusement, sometimes with indignation, often with outrage, of the banking practices of the late twenties. In fact, many of these practices were made ludicrous only by the depression. Loans which would have been perfectly good were made perfectly foolish by the collapse of the borrower's prices or the markets for his goods or the value of the collateral he had posted. The most responsible bankers — those who saw that their debtors were victims of circumstances far beyond their control and sought to help — were often made to look the worst. The bankers yielded, as did others, to the blithe, optimistic, and immoral mood of times but probably not more so. A depression such as that of 1929–32, were it to begin as this is written, would also be damaging to many currently impeccable banking reputations.

However, although the bankers were not unusually foolish in 1929, the banking structure was inherently weak. The weakness was implicit in the large numbers of independent units. When one bank failed, the assets of others were frozen while depositors elsewhere had a pregnant warning to go and ask for their money. Thus one failure led to other failures, and these spread with a domino effect. Even in the best of times local misfortune or isolated mismanagement could start such a chain reaction. (In the first six months of 1929, 346 banks failed in various parts of the country with aggregate deposits of nearly $115 million.)[12] When income, employment, and values fell as the result of a depression bank failures could quickly become epidemic. This happened after 1929. Again it would be hard to imagine a bet-

[12] Compiled from *Federal Reserve Bulletin,* monthly issues, 1929.

ter arrangement for magnifying the effects of fear. The weak destroyed not only the other weak, but weakened the strong. People everywhere, rich and poor, were made aware of the disaster by the persuasive intelligence that their savings had been dest.oyed.

Needless to say, such a banking system, once in the convulsions of failure, had a uniquely repressive effect on the spending of its depositors and the investment of its clients.

4) The dubious state of the foreign balance. This is a familiar story. During the First World War, the United States became a creditor on international account. In the decade following, the surplus of exports over imports which once had paid the interest and principal on loans from Europe continued. The high tariffs, which restricted imports and helped to create this surplus of exports remained. However, history and traditional trading habits also accounted for the persistence of the favorable balance, so called.

Before, payments on interest and principal had in effect been deducted from the trade balance. Now that the United States was a creditor, they were added to this balance. The latter, it should be said, was not huge. In only one year (1928) did the excess of exports over imports come to as much as a billion dollars; in 1923 and 1926 it was only about $375,000,000.[13] Howerer, large or small, this difference had to be covered. Other countries which were buying more than they sold, and had debt payments to make in addition, had somehow to find the means for making up the deficit in their transactions with the United States.

During most of the twenties the difference was covered by cash — i.e., gold payments to the United States — and by new private loans by the United States to other countries.

[13] U.S. Department of Commerce, Bureau of Foreign and Domestic Commerce, *Statistical Abstract of the United States,* 1942.

Most of the loans were to governments — national, state, or municipal bodies — and a large proportion were to Germany and Central and South America. The underwriters' margins in handling these loans were generous; the public took them up with enthusiasm; competition for the business was keen. If unfortunately corruption and bribery were required as competitive instruments, these were used. In late 1927 Juan Leguia, the son of the President of Peru, was paid $450,000 by J. and W. Seligman and Company and the National City Company (the security affiliate of the National City Bank) for his services in connection with a $50,000,000 loan which these houses marketed for Peru.[14] Juan's services, according to later testimony, were of a rather negative sort. He was paid for not blocking the deal. The Chase extended President Machado of Cuba, a dictator with a marked predisposition toward murder, a generous personal line of credit which at one time reached $200,000.[15] Machado's son-in-law was employed by the Chase. The bank did a large business in Cuban bonds. In contemplating these loans, there was a tendency to pass quickly over anything that might appear to the disadvantage of the creditor. Mr. Victor Schoepperle, a vice-president of the National City Company with the responsibility for Latin American loans, made the following appraisal of Peru as a credit prospect:

> Peru: Bad debt record, adverse moral and political risk, bad internal debt situation, trade situation about as satisfactory as that of Chile in the past three years. Natural resources more varied. On economic showing Peru should go ahead rapidly in the next 10 years.[16]

[14] *Stock Exchange Practices,* Report, 1934, pp. 220–21.
[15] *Ibid.,* p. 215.
[16] *Stock Exchange Practices,* Hearings, February–March 1933, Pt. 6, p. 2091 ff.

On such showing the National City Company floated a $15,000,000 loan for Peru, followed a few months later by a $50,000,000 loan, and some ten months thereafter by a $25,-000,000 issue. (Peru did prove a highly adverse political risk. President Leguia, who negotiated the loans, was thrown violently out of office, and the loans went into default.)

In all respects these operations were as much a part of the New Era as Shenandoah and Blue Ridge. They were also just as fragile, and once the illusions of the New Era were dissipated they came as abruptly to an end. This, in turn, forced a fundamental revision in the foreign economic position of the United States. Countries could not cover their adverse trade balance with the United States with increased payments of gold, at least not for long. This meant that they had either to increase their exports to the United States or reduce their imports or default on their past loans. President Hoover and the Congress moved promptly to eliminate the first possibility — that the accounts would be balanced by larger imports — by sharply increasing the tariff. Accordingly, debts, including war debts, went into default and there was a precipitate fall in American exports. The reduction was not vast in relation to total output of the American economy, but it contributed to the general distress and was especially hard on farmers.

5) The poor state of economic intelligence. To regard the people of any time as particularly obtuse seems vaguely improper, and it also establishes a precedent which members of this generation might regret. Yet it seems certain that the economists and those who offered economic counsel in the late twenties and early thirties were almost uniquely perverse. In the months and years following the stock market crash, the burden of reputable economic advice was invariably on the side of measures that would make things worse. In November of 1929, Mr. Hoover announced a cut

in taxes; in the great no-business conferences that followed
he asked business firms to keep up their capital investment
and to maintain wages. Both of these measures were on the
side of increasing spendable income, though unfortunately
they were largely without effect. The tax reductions were
negligible except in the higher income brackets; businessmen who promised to maintain investment and wages, in
accordance with a well-understood convention, considered
the promise binding only for the period within which it was
not financially disadvantageous to do so. As a result investment outlays and wages were not reduced until circumstances would in any case have brought their reduction.

Still, the effort was in the right direction. Thereafter policy
was almost entirely on the side of making things worse.
Asked how the government could best advance recovery, the
sound and responsible adviser urged that the budget be balanced. Both parties agreed on this. For Republicans the
balanced budget was, as ever, high doctrine. But the Democratic Party platform of 1932, with an explicitness which
politicians rarely advise, also called for a "federal budget
annually balanced on the basis of accurate executive estimates within revenues . . ."

A commitment to a balanced budget is always comprehensive. It then meant there could be no increase in government outlays to expand purchasing power and relieve distress. It meant there could be no further tax reduction. But
taken literally it meant much more. From 1930 on the
budget was far out of balance, and balance, therefore, meant
an increase in taxes, a reduction in spending, or both. The
Democratic platform in 1932 called for an "immediate and
drastic reduction of governmental expenditures" to accomplish at least a 25 per cent decrease in the cost of government.

The balanced budget was not a subject of thought. Nor

was it, as often asserted, precisely a matter of faith. Rather it was a formula. For centuries avoidance of borrowing had protected people from slovenly or reckless public house-keeping. Slovenly or reckless keepers of the public purse had often composed complicated arguments to show why balance of income and outlay was not a mark of virtue. Experience had shown that however convenient this belief might seem in the short run, discomfort or disaster followed in the long run. Those simple precepts of a simple world did not hold amid the growing complexities of the early thirties. Mass unemployment in particular had altered the rules. Events had played a very bad trick on people, but almost no one tried to think out the problem anew.

The balanced budget was not the only strait jacket on policy. There was also the bogey of "going off" the gold standard and, most surprisingly, of risking inflation. Until 1932 the United States added formidably to its gold reserves, and instead of inflation the country was experiencing the most violent deflation in the nation's history. Yet every sober adviser saw dangers here, including the danger of runaway price increases. Americans, though in years now well in the past, had shown a penchant for tinkering with the money supply and enjoying the brief but heady joys of a boom in prices. In 1931 or 1932, the danger or even the feasibility of such a boom was nil. The advisers and counselors were not, however, analyzing the danger or even the possibility. They were serving only as the custodians of bad memories.

The fear of inflation reinforced the demand for the balanced budget. It also limited efforts to make interest rates low, credit plentiful (or at least redundant) and borrowing as easy as possible under the circumstances. Devaluation of the dollar was, of course, flatly ruled out. This directly violated the gold standard rules. At best, in such depression times, monetary policy is a feeble reed on which to lean. The current economic clichés did not allow even the use of that frail weapon. And again, these attitudes were above party. Though himself singularly open-minded, Roosevelt was careful not to offend or disturb his followers. In a speech in Brooklyn toward the close of the 1932 campaign, he said:

> The Democratic platform specifically declares, "We advocate a sound currency to be preserved at all hazards." That is plain English. In discussing this platform on July 30, I said, "Sound money is an international necessity, not a domestic consideration for one nation alone." Far up in the Northwest, at Butte, I repeated the pledge . . . In Seattle I reaffirmed my attitude . . . [17]

The following February, Mr. Hoover set forth his view, as often before, in a famous letter to the President-elect:

> It would steady the country greatly if there could be prompt assurance that there will be no tampering or inflation of the currency; that the budget will be unquestionably balanced even if further taxation is necessary; that the Government credit will be maintained by refusal to exhaust it in the issue of securities.[18]

The rejection of both fiscal (tax and expenditure) and monetary policy amounted precisely to a rejection of all affirmative government economic policy. The economic ad-

[17] Lawrence Sullivan, *Prelude to Panic* (Washington: Statesman Press, 1936), p. 20.
[18] William Starr Myers and Walter H. Newton, *The Hoover Administration: A Documented Narrative* (New York: Scribners, 1936), pp. 339–40.

visers of the day had both the unanimity and the authority
to force the leaders of both parties to disavow all the available steps to check deflation and depression. In its own way
this was a marked achievement — a triumph of dogma over
thought. The consequences were profound.

VI

It is in light of the above weaknesses of the economy that
the role of the stock market crash in the great tragedy of the
thirties must be seen. The years of self-depreciation by Wall
Street to the contrary, the role is one of respectable importance. The collapse in securities values affected in the first
instance the wealthy and the well-to-do. But we see that in
the world of 1929 this was a vital group. The members disposed of a large proportion of the consumer income; they
were the source of a lion's share of personal saving and investment. Anything that struck at the spending or investment by this group would of necessity have broad effects on
expenditure and income in the economy at large. Precisely
such a blow was struck by the stock market crash. In addition, the crash promptly removed from the economy the
support that it had been deriving from the spending of stock
market gains.

The stock market crash was also an exceptionally effective
way of exploiting the weaknesses of the corporate structure.
Operating companies at the end of the holding-company
chain were forced by the crash to retrench. The subsequent
collapse of these systems and also of the investment trusts
effectively destroyed both the ability to borrow and the willingness to lend for investment. What have long looked like

purely fiduciary effects were, in fact, quickly translated into declining orders and increasing unemployment.

The crash was also effective in bringing to an end the foreign lending by which the international accounts had been balanced. Now the accounts had, in the main, to be balanced by reduced exports. This put prompt and heavy pressure on export markets for wheat, cotton, and tobacco. Perhaps the foreign loans had only delayed an adjustment in the balance which had one day to come. The stock market crash served nonetheless to precipitate the adjustment with great suddenness at a most unpropitious time. The instinct of farmers who traced their troubles to the stock market was not totally misguided.

Finally, when the misfortune had struck, the attitudes of the time kept anything from being done about it. This, perhaps, was the most disconcerting feature of all. Some people were hungry in 1930 and 1931 and 1932. Others were tortured by the fear that they might go hungry. Yet others suffered the agony of the descent from the honor and respectability that goes with income into poverty. And still others feared that they would be next. Meanwhile everyone suffered from a sense of utter hopelessness. Nothing, it seemed, could be done. And given the ideas which controlled policy, nothing could be done.

Had the economy been fundamentally sound in 1929 the effect of the great stock market crash might have been small. Alternatively, the shock to confidence and the loss of spending by those who were caught in the market might soon have worn off. But business in 1929 was not sound; on the contrary it was exceedingly fragile. It was vulnerable to the kind of blow it received from Wall Street. Those who have emphasized this vulnerability are obviously on strong ground. Yet when a greenhouse succumbs to a hailstorm something more than a purely passive role is normally attributed to the storm. One must accord similar significance to the typhoon which blew out of lower Manhattan in October 1929.

VII

The military historian when he has finished his chronicle is excused. He is not required to consider the chance for a renewal of war with the Indians, the Mexicans, or the Confederacy. Nor will anyone press him to say how such acrimony can be prevented. But economics is taken more seriously. The economic historian, as a result, is invariably asked whether the misfortunes he describes will afflict us again and how they may be prevented.

The task of this book, as suggested on an early page, is only to tell what happened in 1929. It is not to tell whether or when the misfortunes of 1929 will recur. One of the pregnant lessons of that year will by now be plain: it is that very specific and personal misfortune awaits those who presume to believe that the future is revealed to them. Yet, without undue risk, it may be possible to gain from our view of this useful year some insights into the future. We can distinguish, in particular, between misfortunes that could happen again and others which events, many of them in the aftermath of 1929, have at least made improbable. And we can perhaps see a little of the form and magnitude of the remaining peril.

At first glance the least probable of the misadventures of the late twenties would seem to be another wild boom in the stock market with its inevitable collapse. As those days of disenchantment drew to a close, tens of thousands of Americans shook their heads and muttered, "Never again." In every considerable community there are, even now, a few survivors, aged but still chastened, who are still muttering and still shaking their heads. The New Era had no such guardians of sound pessimism.

Also, there are the new government measures and controls. The powers of the Federal Reserve Board — now styled the Board of Governors, the Federal Reserve System — have been strengthened both in relation to the individual Reserve banks and the member banks. Mitchell's defiance of March 1929 is now unthinkable. What was then an act of arrogant but not abnormal individualism would now be regarded as idiotic. The New York Federal Reserve Bank retains a measure of moral authority and autonomy, but not enough to resist any Washington policy. Now also there is power to set margin requirements. If necessary, the speculator can be made to post the full price of the stock he buys. While this may not completely discourage him, it does mean that when the market falls there can be no outsurge of margin calls to force further sales and insure that the liquidation will go through continuing spasms. Finally, the Securities and Exchange Commission is a bar, one hopes effective, to large-scale market manipulation, and it also keeps rein on the devices and the salesmanship by which new speculators are recruited.

Yet, in some respects, the chance for recurrence of a speculative orgy remains good. No one can doubt that the American people remain susceptible to the speculative mood — to the conviction that enterprise can be attended by unlimited rewards in which they, individually, were meant to share. A rising market can still bring the reality of riches. This, in turn, can draw more and more people to participate. The government preventatives and controls are ready. In the hands of a determined government their efficacy cannot be doubted. There are, however, a hundred reasons why a government will determine not to use them. In our democracy an election is in the offing even on the day after an election. The avoidance of depression and the prevention of unemployment have become for the politician the most critical of all questions of public policy. Action to break up a boom must always be weighed against the chance that it will cause unemployment at a politically inopportune moment. Booms, it must be noted, are not stopped until after they have started. And after they have started the action will always look, as it did to the frightened men in the Federal Reserve Board in February 1929, like a decision in favor of immediate as against ultimate death. As we have seen, the immediate death not only has the disadvantage of being immediate but of identifying the executioner.

The market will not go on a speculative rampage without some rationalization. But during any future boom some newly rediscovered virtuosity of the free enterprise system will be cited. It will be pointed out that people are justified in paying the present prices — indeed, almost any price — to have an equity position in the system. Among the first to accept these rationalizations will be some of those responsible for invoking the controls. They will say firmly that controls are not needed. The newspapers, some of them, will agree and speak harshly of those who think action might be in order. They will be called men of little faith.[19]

VIII

A new adventure in stock market speculation sometime in the future followed by another collapse would not have the same effect on the economy as in 1929. Whether it would

---

[19] In warning in 1969 of the then current speculation I managed to attract, in a modest way, this epithet.

show the economy to be fundamentally sound or unsound is something, unfortunately, that will not be wholly evident until after the event. There can be no question, however, that many of the points of extreme weakness exposed in 1929 or soon thereafter have since been substantially strengthened. The distribution of income is no longer quite so lopsided. Between 1929 and 1948 the share of total personal income going to the 5 per cent of the population with the highest income dropped from nearly a third to less than a fifth of the total. Between 1929 and 1950 the share of all family income which was received as wages, salaries, pensions, and unemployment compensation increased from approximately 61 per cent to approximately 71 per cent. This is the income of everyday people. Although dividends, interest, and rent, the income characteristically of the well-to-do, increased in total amount, the share dropped from just over 22 to just over 12 per cent of total family personal income.[20] In ensuing years the improvement in income distribution tapered off and slightly reversed itself. It remains far better than in the twenties.

Similarly after 1929, the great investment trust promotions were folded up and put away, although eventually they were replaced in part, and alas, by mutual and offshore funds, Equity Funding and the Real Estate Investment Trusts, which became the casualties of the post-1970 collapse. However, the SEC, aided by the bankruptcy laws, flattened out the great utility holding company pyramids. Federal insurance of bank deposits, even to this day, has not been given full credit for the revolution that it has worked in the nation's banking structure. With this one piece of legislation the fear which operated so efficiently to transmit weakness

[20] These data are from Goldsmith, *et al.*, "Size of Distribution of Income," pp. 16, 18.

was dissolved. As a result one grievous defect of the old system, by which failure begot failure, was cured. Rarely has so much been accomplished by a single law.

The problem of the foreign balance is much changed from what it was twenty-five years ago. Now the United States finds itself with a propensity to buy or spend far more than it sells and receives.

Finally, there has been a modest accretion of economic knowledge. A developing depression would not now be met with a fixed determination to make it worse. Without question, ceremonial conferences would be assembled at the White House. We would see an explosion of reassurance and incantation. Many would urge waiting and hoping as the best policy. Not again, however, would people suppose that the best policy would be — as Secretary Mellon so infelicitously phrased it — to "liquidate labor, liquidate stocks, liquidate the farmers, liquidate real estate." [21] Our determination to deal firmly and adequately with a serious depression is still to be tested. But there is still a considerable difference between a failure to do enough that is right and a determination to do much that is wrong.

Other weaknesses in the economy have been corrected. The much maligned farm program provides a measure of security for farm income and therewith for spending by farmers. Unemployment compensation accomplishes the same result, if still inadequately, for labor. The remainder of the social security system — pensions and public assistance — helps protect the income and consequently the expenditures of yet other segments of the population. The tax system is a far better servant of stability than it was in 1929. An angry god may have endowed capitalism with inherent

[21] Quoted by Herbert Hoover, *Memoirs*, p. 30.

contradictions. But at least as an afterthought he was kind enough to make social reform surprisingly consistent with improved operation of the system.

IX

Yet all this reinforcement notwithstanding, it would be unwise to expose the economy to the shock of another major speculative collapse. Some of the new reinforcements might buckle. Fissures might open at other new and perhaps unexpected places. Even the quick withdrawal from the economy of the spending that comes from stock market gains might be damaging. Any collapse, even though the further consequences were small, would not be good for the public reputation of Wall Street.

Wall Street, in recent times, has become, as a learned phrase has it, very "public relations conscious." Since a speculative collapse can only follow a speculative boom, one might expect that Wall Street would lay a heavy hand on any resurgence of speculation. The Federal Reserve would be asked by bankers and brokers to lift margins to the limit; it would be warned to enforce the requirement sternly against those who might try to borrow on their own stocks and bonds in order to buy more of them. The public would be warned sharply and often of the risks inherent in buying stocks for the rise. Those who persisted, nonetheless, would have no one to blame but themselves. The position of the Stock Exchange, its members, the banks, and the financial community in general would be perfectly clear and as well protected in the event of a further collapse as sound public relations allow.

As noted, all this might logically be expected. However, it did not happen in the go-go years of the late sixties and immediately after — the years of the performance funds and the conglomerate explosion — nor will it come to pass. This is not because the instinct for self-preservation in Wall Street is poorly developed. On the contrary, it is probably normal and may be above. But now, as throughout history, financial capacity and political perspicacity are inversely correlated. Long-run salvation by men of business has never been highly regarded if it means disturbance of orderly life and convenience in the present. So inaction will be advocated in the present even though it means deep trouble in the future. Here, at least equally with communism, lies the threat to capitalism. It is what causes men who know that things are going quite wrong to say that things are fundamentally sound.

INDEX

Index

50n., 51n., 55n., 56n., 58n., 59n., 61n., 63n.

Securities and Exchange Commission in the Matter of Richard Whitney, et al., 161n., 162n., 164n.

Securities market. *See* Stock market

Seligman and Company, J. and W., 181

Senate, 40; senators' salaries, 157–58

Senate Committee on Banking and Currency, 156

   Stock Exchange Practices, Hearings: 38n., 60n., 64n., 73n., 132n., 148n., 149n., 150n., 156n., 158n., 181n.

   Report: 31n., 51n., 67n., 78n., 79n., 147n., 148n., 149n., 153n., 154n., 181n.

Shenandoah Corporation, 61, 62, 64, 67, 124, 142, 182

Shermar Corporation, 148–49

Short selling, 148–49, 157, 166

Simmons Company, 77

Simmons, Edward H. H., 64n., 102, 156

Sinclair Consolidated Oil Company, 148, 158

Sinclair, Harry F., 83, 148, 158

Sloan, Alfred P., Jr., 121, 138

Smith, Alfred E., 13, 15, 131–32

Smith, Bernard E., 158, 164

Social Security, 192

Socialists, 125, 155

Solvay American Investment Corporation, 64

South America, loans, 181

South Sea Bubble, 7, 46, 49, 80, 170

Sparling, Earl, 40n.

Speculation, 11, 67–68, 107; boom begins in earnest, 11–12; brokers' loans index of, 20–21; characteristics of speculative periods, 4, 6–7, 11–12, 18, 24, 46, 169–70, 189–90, collapse of, 90; control of, 24–25, 32; and Coolidge, 26; devices of, 18–22; estimated participation in, 78; exposure of, 135; and Federal Reserve, 33–34, 42; Florida boom, 3–4, 6–7, 11; and Hoover, 16; immunizing effect of collapse, 171, 190; industrial stocks focus of, 7n.; reasons for orgy, 169–70; responsibility for

crash, 169; safeguards against 188–89; and Warburg, 72. *See also* Margin trading, Speculators, Stock Market

Speculators, 13–14, 18, 80–81, 83, 87, 96, 104, 106, 113, 134–35, 147, 150; causing crash, 90–92; estimated number of, 77–78; investigation of famous operators, 158; margin calls, 36–37, 95, 99, 108, 110, 120, 123; panic, 100; suicides, 128, 130–32

Spokesman–Review, Spokane, 81

Standard Oil of New Jersey, 31, 63, 135–36, 141

Standard Statistics Company, 73

State Street Investment Corporation, 56

Stevens, Eugene M., 106

Stock exchanges, Boston, 49; Buffalo, 100; Chicago, 49, 100; out-of-town exchanges, 67, 123; panic, 100; regulation of (SEC), 166

Stock exchange firms, 78, 107; exhaustion, 113, 116; failures, 108, 116, 159; moral standards of, 159; sponsors of investment trusts, 50; transoceanic brokerage, 81–82. *See also* Brokers

Stock Exchange Practices. *See* Senate Committee on Banking and Currency

Stock Market

   Babson break, 86 big operators, 13–14, 80–81; Black Thursday, 98–105, 110

   Boom: survived Florida, 7; rising prices in twenties, 7–8; March 1928, 12–13; June 1928, 15; election forecasts, 15; post-election boom, 16–17; February 1929 setback, 34; March nervousness, 35–38; summer spurt, 66

   Bull market ended, 84; center of immorality, 155–56, 158; impersonal market, 13, 111; *1930–32,* 141–42; October prelude *1929,* 90–98; official optimism, sober predictions, 70–74; organized support, 95–96, 98, 100–102, 110, 118, 122, 126; panic, 98–100; predominance of, 74–81; reassurance, 106, 118, 126 (see also Incanta-